Dublin from 1970 to 1990

The Making of Dublin City

SERIES EDITORS
Joseph Brady and Anngret Simms (to volume 5), University College Dublin
Ruth McManus (from volume 5), Dublin City University

Dublin from 1970 to 1990

to 1990

THE CITY TRANSFORMED

Joseph Brady

FOUR COURTS PRESS

Set in AGaramondPro 11pt/14pt by
Carrigboy Typesetting Services for
FOUR COURTS PRESS LTD
7 Malpas Street, Dublin 8, Ireland
www.fourcourtspress.ie
and in North America for
FOUR COURTS PRESS
c/o IPG, 814 North Franklin Street, Chicago, IL 60610

© Joseph Brady and Four Courts Press 2022

A catalogue record for this title is available
from the British Library.

ISBN 978-1-84682-986-4 hbk
ISBN 978-1-84682-980-2 pbk

Printed in Spain by GraphyCems, Navarra.

Contents

CONTENTS

Abbreviations

CBD	central business district
CDL	Coal Distributors Limited
CHDDA	Custom House Docklands Development Authority
CIÉ	Córas Iompair Éireann
CSO	Central Statistics Office
DADC	Dublin Artisans' Dwellings Company
DART	Dublin Area Rapid Transit
DDDA	Dublin Docklands Development Authority
DRRTS	Dublin Rail Rapid Transit Study
DTA	Dublin Transportation Authority
DTS	Dublin Transportation Study
EC	European Communities
ECP	Euro Car Parks
EEC	European Economic Community
ERDO	East Region Development Organisation
ESB	Electricity Supply Board
GPO	General Post Office
HMSO	Her Majesty's Stationery Office
ICTU	Irish Congress of Trade Unions
IDA	Industrial Development Agency
IFSC	International Financial Services Centre
IIRS	Institute for Industrial Research Standards
ILAC	Irish Life Assurance Centre
ITGWU	Irish Transport and General Workers' Union
LPG	liquid petroleum gas
NABCO	National Association of Building Co-operatives
NBST	National Board for Science and Technology
NEDO	National Economic Development Office
NUI	National University of Ireland
OPEC	Organization of the Petroleum Exporting Countries
OPW	Office of Public Works
OS	Ordnance Survey
PMPA	Private Motorists' Protection Association
PUS	public utility society

QBC	Quality Bus Corridors
RIAI	Royal Institute of the Architects of Ireland
TCD	Trinity College Dublin
UCD	University College Dublin
UDS	Universal Department Stores
USSR	Union of Soviet Socialist Republics

Acknowledgments

This series of books has explored the growth and development of Dublin from the earliest times. With this volume we arrive at a time I remember, so the research process is somewhat different and more challenging. Inevitably my view of the city is influenced by my own experiences of the times, both as a citizen and as a young academic beginning what turned out to be a lifelong exploration. In writing the book I was conscious of the danger of slipping into memoir, and I hope that I have managed to avoid this and that the analysis offered in these pages is solidly based on the facts. One of the interesting aspects of undertaking the research for this book was to be reminded of events and processes that have faded from public memory but were significant at the time and which, in their own ways, helped to shape the Dublin of today. A variety of sources were important in trying to develop an understanding of the city during these years and these will emerge in the pages that follow. You will see that images were particularly important because one of the purposes of this book is to give a sense of how the city looked. What did the centre of Dublin look like, what impression did a walk along its streets convey? I am particularly grateful, therefore, to my mentor Dr Tony Parker for many of the photographs used here. He introduced me to the idea of capturing a changing landscape by regular visits to the same locations, but I hardly realized at the time how important his images would be and, indeed, the ones that I took at a later period.

This book was written during the restrictions that were made necessary by the Covid pandemic. This restricted access to archives and libraries and made online resources all the more valuable and important. Discussions with friends and colleagues across Zoom and other platforms had to replace more convivial discussion fora. I am especially thankful to Professor Hugh Campbell, Professor Gerald Mills and Professor Bryan Fanning for their help. I am also most grateful to the National University of Ireland for a grant towards the cost of publication. We felt that the time had come to show the city in colour and NUI's help was crucial in allowing us to achieve this.

As ever I am immensely grateful to my editor, Professor Ruth McManus, for her insights and her close attention to detail. This book has benefitted immensely from the hours that she has devoted to reading, commenting and advising.

Four Courts Press continue to be our trusted partners in this series and I am ever grateful to Martin Fanning and Sam Tranum for all that has been done to get this volume to press. I also appreciate greatly the work done by Anthony Tierney in sales and marketing and for ensuring that the volumes continue to be available. Four Courts Press produce books to the highest standards and they make a vital contribution to the academic world.

My deepest thanks, though, must go to Anne for her continuing and unfailing encouragement and support. Without her, neither this book nor any of the others would have been written.

Series editor's introduction

Although our exploration of Dublin reaches into relatively recent times with this volume, the city that is explored is at the same time both familiar and yet quite distant to the contemporary reader. The country faced two oil crises in the 1970s. Long queues outside petrol stations provided a stark reminder that the country and city were inextricably linked to the global economy, with all of its geopolitical implications. In the same decade, Ireland continued its political modernization as it finally joined the EEC in 1973. This increasing openness was also visible on the streets of the city, where new retailers came on the scene, while new ways of doing business and new thinking about how the city should operate were playing out. For the first time in the 1970s, Ireland experienced net immigration: in other words, more people were coming in than leaving. Dublin continued to attract population growth, which was seen in ongoing suburban growth and an extending commuter belt.

In this volume we see the impacts of the changing retail offering on both city and suburbs. While the previous volume in the series, *Dublin in the 1950s and 1960s: cars, shops and suburbs*, introduced the first purpose-built shopping centre at Stillorgan, Joe Brady explores the evolution of the concept in some detail here. We learn how the centres of the 1970s and 1980s were laid out, the choice of anchor tenants and the various ways in which they sought to entice customers. In many ways, retailing followed the expanding suburban population, with significant developments at Northside and Donaghmede, but also in slightly more established areas like Crumlin, Rathfarnham and Nutgrove. The lengthy wait for services in the new town of Tallaght finally ended with the opening of The Square in 1990, the first of the new regional-level shopping centres, which would be followed by Blanchardstown and Liffey Valley. As out-of-town shopping became increasingly popular, the centre fought back. As we shall see, increasing levels of pedestrianization and the offering of suburban-style experiences within the centre – as at the Irish Life and ILAC malls – were among the efforts of the city centre to adapt to the challenge.

Transportation policy was an ongoing issue, with increasing car dependence and difficulties in providing adequate public-transport alternatives in the ever-expanding low-density suburbs. The city was choked with cars. One solution was the introduction of paid on-street parking as well as the development of purpose-built multi-storey car parks.

As the excellent range of photos in this volume demonstrates, a visitor to Dublin in the 1970s and early 1980s would have encountered significant urban decay and dereliction at the heart of the city. Much of this was the legacy of socio-economic changes that have been discussed in previous volumes. Large 'bomb site'-style car parks were available well into the 1980s on sites close to the centre that had been cleared but remained unbuilt. These empty sites were the outcome of previous slum clearances, together with the removal of industry either to the suburbs or overseas. Most would be replaced as part of the urban-renewal policies of the mid-1980s and into the 1990s, when the so-called Celtic Tiger saw extensive development in the city once again.

The period of this volume covers the start of urban-renewal efforts and considers the policy background to the changes that took place along the quays, in the docklands and in Temple Bar. In addition to the significant physical changes this wrought on the city, social and economic changes also resulted. For the first time, purpose-built apartments were provided for the private market, bringing about demographic change. The popularity of city-centre living, at least for a young and mobile workforce, was novel in a city that had been experiencing mass suburbanization for more than half a century.

This book is the first in the series to have a specific chapter considering Dublin's environmental issues. Those who lived through this era will have no difficulty recalling the 'whiffy Liffey', which was immortalized in the 1980 Bagatelle hit song 'Summer in Dublin'. The smogs of the early 1980s are perhaps less well remembered. However, the plague of poor air quality was an important issue, which receives deserved attention here. Finally, proposals to build an oil refinery in Dublin Bay may have faded from public memory, but battles over the future of Dublin Bay continue to the present day, despite its designation as a UNESCO biosphere reserve.

Readers will find many echoes and resonances with recent experiences in this volume, which was completed during the Covid-19 pandemic. The challenges of the pandemic have thrown a spotlight on where we live, with an increasing recognition of the concept of liveability and an awareness that access to nature and to open space is of fundamental importance. There has been a return to modes of transport that had been in decline. The bicycle in particular has seen a resurgence in popularity, leading to often heated discussions about the need for cycle lanes and a challenge to car dominance. More generally there has been a rethinking of how we use our public spaces, how cities and towns can be more welcoming, and how space can be used for the good of the many rather than the few. Experiments with new forms of pedestrianization, outdoor dining, and increased greening of the city have formed part of the response to the latest challenge facing the city.

The full implications of the past eighteen months have yet to play out in the geography of the city. Prophets of doom may focus on the deepening housing crisis, reduced demands for office space and a loss of retail vitality. Perhaps this book will give some cause for hope, as it explores how the economic adjustments of the 1970s and 1980s saw vacancy and dereliction give way to urban renewal. Similarly, as we address increasingly challenging environmental questions in light of global climate change, can we learn from the debates around smog in the early 1980s? One thing that will be evident to readers of this series is that, despite its many ups and downs, Dublin is a resilient city that has weathered many storms throughout its long history. We hope that you will enjoy this latest addition to the series, that it will jog memories, inspire insights and give some hope for the future.

RUTH McMANUS

In Dublin's fair city

Inflation was high as the 1970s began. It was not the only thing that was of concern to the citizens. The population lived in the shadow of nuclear war and every household had a copy of *Bás Beatha*, a hopelessly optimistic manual for surviving a nuclear attack. The Soviet Union was certainly aware of Dublin. It even went to the trouble of stealing OS maps and indicating buildings of importance. There might have been some comfort in the fact that very little in Dublin was highlighted, except for the fairly obvious docklands and some public buildings.

Taking 1970 as a base, the consumer price index rose by 43.3 per cent in the period to the end of 1973. The property market was doing very well. A feature in the *Irish Times* in May 1970 suggested that annual returns of between 6.5 per cent and 8.5 per cent were available for new offices and shopping centres. It was said that 'property has been accepted by the investor, whether

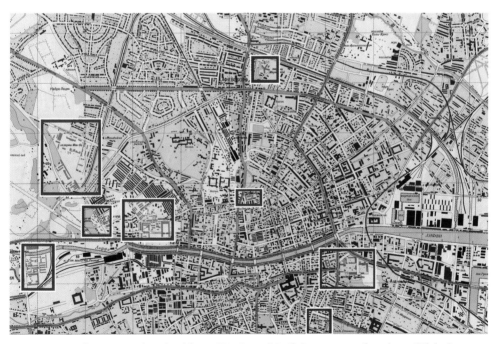

1 Extract from USSR plan of Dublin. USSR General Staff plan, 1:10,000, four sheets. While the map is dated '1980' the content dates from the early 1970s. The mauve shading (highlighted), indicates 'government or academic facilities'; the green indicates 'military objects'.

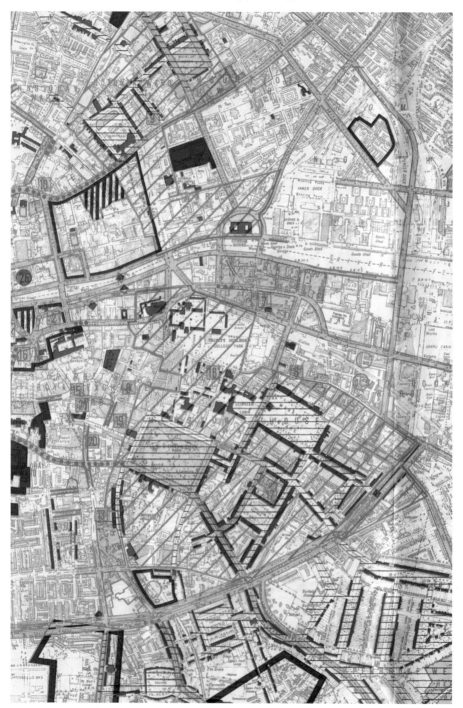

2 Main area with 'structures for preservation'.
(Extract from Dublin Development Plan, 1971, map 2.)

private or institutional, as a first-class security containing a built-in hedge against inflation'. So much so, it was suggested that there was room for more international investors in the Irish market (*Irish Times*, 23 May 1970, p. A9). By the end of 1973, it seemed that there was a mini-boom in Dublin and, for example, there was little new empty office space available (*Irish Times*, 7 September 1973). Property was where those with money were prepared to invest. Those seeking mortgages were experiencing a different story; personal money was scarce and interest rates were high. However, it would be wrong to suggest that this boom in the office sector and in the commercial-property market generally was being experienced equally across Dublin.

Map 2 of the Development Plan produced by Dublin Corporation in 1971 revealed a city centre that faced many challenges. The maps showed the battleground for the various land uses. There were the planned roads – this was still the era of trying to accommodate the car. In red were shown the areas for conservation; the idea that the city would be actively involved in preserving parts of the urban landscape, mostly Georgian, was new. Given what had happened in the nineteenth century with the gradual but persistent tenementation of so much of the city, it came as no surprise that this was heavily concentrated in the south-eastern sector. This was where the best-preserved urban landscape existed. Still, the map recognized that there was a smaller but significant zone in the north city that reached from Parnell Square to Mountjoy Square. This included Parnell Square, Mountjoy Square, Gardiner Place, much of Eccles Street, Henrietta Street, part of Dominick Street Lower and scattered individual buildings. Whatever about the chances for the south-east, in the north city the developers had been enthusiastic in their demolition attempts, and preservation here would require more than simple designation; decay and dereliction were widespread.

However, the viewer's eye is inevitably drawn to what were called 'obsolete' areas and 'redevelopment' areas, coloured in shades of purple on the map. These were found in most of the centre, except the favoured south-east. They were extensive, occupying most of the north city centre from the quays to Parnell Street. They existed along South Great George's Street and south into Camden Street. There was a large area along the north and south quays to the west of Church Street and a similar area on George's and City quays to the east of Butt Bridge. Both zones occupied a great deal of the city centre that people and visitors saw – the main areas of the city, not just the back streets. No Dubliner should have been surprised by this picture. Flora Mitchell had captured a city in genteel decay during the 1960s, and the subsequent decade

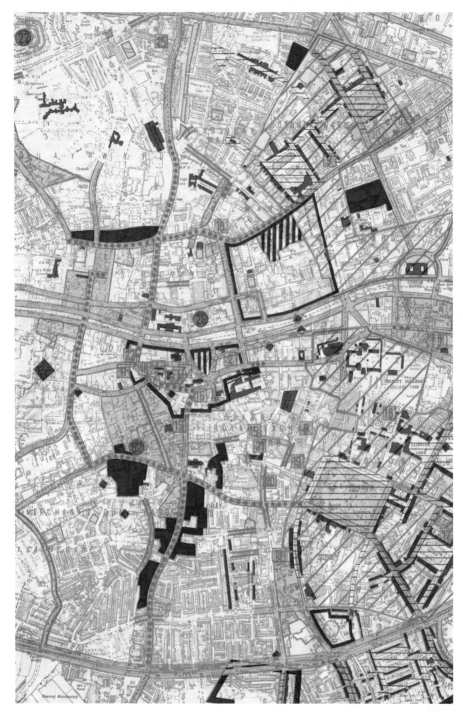

3 Main area with 'obsolete' and 'redevelopment areas'.
(Extract from Dublin Development Plan, 1971, map 2.)

37 Local shopping provision at the western (Coolock) end of Tonlegee Road, early 1970s.

The centre might have seen Simon Dee as a suitable draw for the opening but Superquinn decided that The Riordans made more sense for them! It was an interesting distinction, the former appealing to an outward-looking, modern society, the latter to a traditional and distinctively non-urban society.

The centre was located on a 3.4ha site with parking for 731 cars on two sides and about 11,700 sq. m devoted to shopping. The Corporation swimming pool, with an area of 930 sq. m, was in the roof space. The range across the 56 shops was quite wide and shoppers could explore ladies', gents' and children's fashions and footwear, toy shops, butchers, bakery and confectionery stores, a DIY shop, an electrical store, newsagents, record store, more accessories and services such as ladies' hairdressing, television rental, a building society, bank, optician and dental surgery, together with the obligatory coffee shop. The original open mall design was enclosed in 1975 when it was extended by 1,400 sq. m. What Northside did not have was many of the stores to be found in the city centre. A regional centre needed to replicate (if not replace) the offerings in the city centre and despite its size and location, this did not occur. The drapers O'Reilly and Company of North Earl Street took a large unit and there were branches of Best's, the men's outfitters and Connolly's and Kenny's shoe stores, but none of these could be described as high-end retailing. Despite it not posing a significant threat to the city centre, the centre did quite well and quickly became integrated into the local economy. Its impact on local shopping provision, provided earlier both by Dublin Corporation and private developers, was less than might have been expected and much survived by providing lower order and more frequently purchased goods.

Northside shopping centre was well located with respect to the new developments along the northern edge of the city but there was a need and an opportunity to provide for the growing population to the east, in and around Kilbarrack. This locality had been one of the few remaining unbuilt areas within the realm of Dublin Corporation and been the subject of intense competition between the Corporation and private developers. As discussed in a previous volume, the development atmosphere was febrile and it resulted in legal actions. This meant that building was rapid and intense and there was very quickly a large population that needed shopping services. It would have made best sense to treat the area holistically and to put in a hierarchy of provision. There were enough people in the hinterland to sustain this but achieving it would have required a degree of co-operation between developers and a degree of co-ordination between them and the Corporation which did not occur. The result was sub-optimal, with two centres in close proximity.

Kilbarrack and Donaghmede

The first centre to be developed was in Kilbarrack. The location chosen was close to Kilbarrack Road, the final element in the west-to-east artery that connected Finglas to the coast. It was also close to the Howth Road, the main artery along the coast and adjacent to the railway line, though at the time this was only a limited commuter line. As was usual, there were puff pieces in the main newspapers to celebrate the opening of the centre (*Evening Herald*, 1 December 1971). It was a staggered opening, with many of the units not in place before January 1972 but there was a desire to capitalize on the Christmas market by getting up and running in December. Unusually, the developers had undertaken some locational analysis and had engaged the Copenhagen Institute of Centre Planning as consultants on the project to produce a profile of the likely demand and character of the shoppers. This told them that they had some 20,000 people or 5,000 families in the immediate area, which was about the same as Northside. They decided to concentrate on local provision and limited their expected hinterland to about 2.4km around the centre.

38 Opening advertisement for Kilbarrack shopping centre.
(*Evening Herald*, 1 December 1971, p. 9.)

Northside was over 3km away as the crow flies but across the increasingly busy Malahide Road and there was no indication that they would have seen themselves in competition with it. In fact, they reckoned that many shoppers would walk (see the commentary on consumer behaviour below). This probably reflected the position with car ownership at the time but all of the forecasts suggested that this would grow and that people would increasingly want to use their cars to shop. They provided only 170 parking spaces but they believed that this would be sufficient for shoppers from Howth, Malahide, Portmarnock and Clontarf.

The design was different to what had been built in Dublin to that point. It was all on one level, air-conditioned, heated when necessary and fully enclosed – a first for Ireland, they claimed. There was community engagement in that the developers offered the locals the opportunity to use the concourse for meetings and other activities while they awaited the arrival of community services. They even suggested that the high-quality marble floor would be suitable for dancing. It was much smaller than Northside, with only about one-third of that centre's floor space. Granted it was close to the Edenmore shopping parade, which was relatively new too, but the latter was a conventional street-facing run of shops at the time. The anchor supermarket in the Kilbarrack shopping centre's 3,800 sq. m of shopping, at the time, was a Power supermarket combined with a Penneys store selling clothes, both companies being part of the Associated British Foods empire. This unit of almost 2,000 sq. m dominated the centre and occupied one side of the main concourse. An unusual selling point was that it provided a parking area for prams and, by keeping display units to under 1.5m in height, it permitted mothers to keep an eye on their pram from any part of the store. There were twenty units, a standard mix of middle-order goods – some clothes shops, an electrical store, a DIY store, a record store, newsagent, hairdresser, a branch of Ulster Bank and, of course, a coffee shop. In 1983, the supermarket was combined with the clothes shop and another unit to produce the Crazy Prices anchor, with 2,300 sq. m.

The Donaghmede shopping centre was only a stone's throw away from the Kilbarrack centre, no more than 1km away by road but on the northern side of Kilbarrack Road. It proposed to serve a population of about 6,000 families with a centre of about 7,400 sq. m and was therefore in direct competition with Kilbarrack. It was officially opened on 30 October 1973 but elements of it had been in operation for almost a year previously and many of the units had individual openings. The developer was the Gallagher Group, who had built 1,650 houses in the locality – 400 at Grangemore, 800 at Donaghmede and 450 at Swan's Nest – and might have felt that they understood the area well, especially as there were plans at the time for another 1,600 houses nearby. This was a more traditional build than Kilbarrack. It was over two floors with an open courtyard. It seemed that those living north of Kilbarrack Road were a hardier breed but they were expected to use their cars in larger numbers; 900 parking spaces were provided. This time the anchor was H. Williams

H.Williams open their
16ᵗʰ Supermarket in Dublin next week

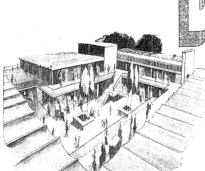

Donaghmede

SHOPPING CENTRE

Now! Shoppers in the Raheny area are to have their own H. Williams Supermarket for Super Savings, great variety and Green Shield Stamps. The beautiful big new H. Williams Supermarket at Donaghmede Shopping Centre carries a complete range of HW brands and all leading national brands. Shop in comfort and confidence. There's ample parking outside and everything arranged for your convenience inside.
Plus great bargains in every aisle. See for yourself next week.

H.Williams ■SUPERMARKETS

Dundrum, Killester, Santry (Lorcan Ave.), Dun Laoghaire, Clonkeen Rd., Henry Street, Churchtown, Terenure, Lower Baggot Street, Sandymount, Rathfarnham, Rathmines, Mount Merrion, Tallaght, Finglas.

GROCERIES, MEAT & POULTRY, WINES & SPIRITS, DELICATESSEN, HEALTH & BEAUTY, HARDWARE, HOUSEWARES, DRAPERY, TOYS,

39 Advertisement at opening of Donaghmede shopping centre.
(*Evening Herald*, 27 October 1973.)

who had standalone units in Santry and Killester. The full-page advertisement announcing their opening in Donaghmede, which they placed in Raheny (*Evening Herald*, 29 October 1973, p. 7), was less effusive than others. The provision of Green Shield stamps was seen as a major draw, as was the availability of HW brands and all leading national brands. There was a nod towards bargains in every aisle, but it was rather low-key. It occupied just over 2,000 sq. m while Universal Department Stores (UDS) had about the same. UDS were a new arrival, without a presence elsewhere but a department store was a distinctive feature not found in other centres of this size. As befitting a department store, they offered 'everything under the sun', including clothing, footwear, furniture, carpets, floor coverings and toys. Neither they nor W&L Crowe, builders' providers and DIY, lasted long and in 1975, they were replaced by Dunnes Stores. This had been Crowe's first experience of a retail store and they had hoped to capitalize on an upsurge in DIY enthusiasm in the new housing areas around. This was Dunnes first excursion into the northern suburbs and the *Irish Independent* seemed to think it would be a different experience since 'the major difference between shopping centres on both sides of the Liffey is that on the south side they are located on major arterial roads while on the northside they are tucked away in the heart of major housing areas' (1 February 1975, p. 3). This comment suggest that the *Irish Independent* had limited experience of the northside! In addition to shopping there was 1,100 sq. m of office space and the Donaghmede Inn, a spacious pub. As well as the usual mix of low-order and middle-order stores, this centre attracted some interest from established stores in the city centre such as Nicholl's of Exchequer Street, a large and long-established drapers, and from A.F. Byrne of Capel Street, a sportswear shop. There was also a range of shops that was now appearing in the various centres, though not present in the city centre. Berney Mastervision provided televisions from seventeen stores nationwide while Kavanagh's men's fashions were also in Northside and Ballymun (Seven Towers).

Donaghmede began to eclipse the Kilbarrack centre almost immediately. It was quickly extended to 11,100 sq. m and by the middle 1980s the centre's footprint had grown again to over 12,700 sq. m. By the end of the 1980s, the main anchor was a large Dunnes Stores, with 6,200 sq. m of retail space, half of the centre, selling groceries, drapery, hardware and alcohol.

The reasons why Donaghmede grew and Kilbarrack did not are unclear. Both were centrally located to their population and there was no significant difference in accessibility. Kilbarrack had better access to the rail service but at the time of opening this would not have been a competitive advantage. It would have had an effect had the DART been in operation. On the face of it, Kilbarrack had the more interesting and comfortable centre but it was smaller and the range of shops was narrower. It could have been the choice of supermarket or the availability of a 'department stores' of sorts that worked to Donaghmede's advantage. As time went on, the availability of parking space must have become an element. Donaghmede's superiority was assured when Dunnes combined the grocery, hardware and drapery provision and it was the seventh largest planned centre in Dublin by 1990.

Crumlin

Crumlin shopping centre arrived in 1974 and was large enough to make the top ten in 1990 with just over 9,800 sq. m of net retail space. It joined Phibsborough as an insertion into a well-established residential area. Although there had been housing schemes by Guinness and the Dublin Artisans' Dwelling Company, it was Dublin Corporation's very large housing schemes of the late 1930s that

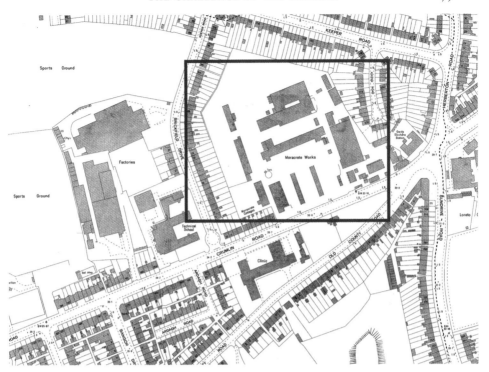

40 The Crumlin shopping centre site prior to redevelopment.
(Ordnance Survey plan, 1:1,100, Sheet 3263-22, 1972.)

gave the area its character. By the 1970s the area had moved into maturity and people would have had well established shopping patterns. There was not an obvious need for a shopping centre but planning permission was obtained in 1972. The local traders objected and an oral planning appeal was held on 17 May 1972 in the Custom House. The objections crystallized around a fear that the local traders would be put out of business by the new centre, which was large by the standards of the time. It was argued that there were 400 traders in the immediate locality and that all local needs were already well met. What was needed instead was more housing. There were also objections that the increased traffic the centre would generate would be detrimental to the local environment and the safety of its inhabitants, especially schoolchildren. The developers countered by saying that their research indicated that many in the locality shopped in the city centre and the new development would improve convenience. They also argued that 'other areas' had shown that new centres often generated additional business for established retail units, though they did not name these areas. It would have been very interesting to learn where these places were located, if they existed. The developers also noted the 'stringent' planning conditions which, inter alia, related to traffic management, the environment and community engagement. Moreover, a swimming pool was promised as part of the complex (*Irish Independent*, 18 May 1972, p. 13).

The objections did not succeed and permission was given by the minister, Bobby Molloy, in September 1972. In April 1973, it was announced that finance would be provided by the Investment Bank of Ireland and the *Irish Independent* reported that the new centre was 'located in the midst of a vast housing area served by scattered local shopping parades and out of reach of the major south city shopping centres at Stillorgan, Rathfarnham'. That was certainly true but car ownership in the locality was below the city average so filling the 700 car-parking spaces would require a big hinterland. They claimed a catchment area of Crumlin, Drimnagh, Inchicore, Kimmage, Dolphin's Barn and Walkinstown, with a population 'in excess of 78,500 within a one mile radius' (*Irish Independent*, 6 April 1973, p. A1). This was probably a significant overestimate but there was certainly a large pool of potential customers. The location was good as well. Built on the site of Moracrete Ltd, it was at the focal point of two major arteries in the area – Crumlin Road and Sundrive Road – and there was a reasonably good bus service.

The centre also promised to be attractive. It would be fully enclosed (competing with Kilbarrack for the accolade of being 'first') with heating and air conditioning and as well as high-design values there would be a 25m swimming pool, a pub (which was unusual), a crèche, public toilets and telephones. The latter were important features and worth mentioning when getting a private phone in Dublin could take in excess of five years. This social provision had been a key element in the promotion of the centre during the planning process. Following the granting of permission, the developers stated that the anchors would be a supermarket and a department store – the standard mix for a centre of this size. However, all of the stores would open directly onto the main concourse – there would be no conventional storefronts. The letting agent, John Finnegan of Finnegan Menton, likened it to Moore Street, the Flea Market in Athens, 'the Casbah' and some of the developments on the Costa del Sol.

> These places have great atmosphere because generally speaking, the dimensions are easily comprehensible in human terms, narrow communicating corridors do not overwhelm the bodies which use them and while the commercial aspect is paramount in them all, they are essentially venues for people.

These are some of the concepts which inspired the Crumlin Centre. Sure we want people to shop there, but we hope that they can also relax in a pleasing landscaped environment, have a drink in the pub or a swim in the pool. In other words we are accepting the point that shopping is a vital part of communal living, and a means whereby people meet, communicate and enjoy social inter course. Just having a cup of coffee with a neighbour while the children are being looked after safely in the crèche can provide a necessary 'break' from the domestic grind for the housewife.

(Irish Independent, 15 September 1972, p. 21)

The official opening was on 19 September 1974, with Gay Byrne attracting a crowd of between 8,000 and 10,000 people to the event. The new centre was described in large advertising features that appeared on 26 September with the slogan 'Crumlin Shopping Centre brings down your cost of living'. The reality was not quite as promised – there were 40 stores providing a wide range of goods and services but there were individual shopfronts, which made the mall rather narrow. There was no department store but, as other centres were finding, it was difficult to persuade such stores that the days of the dominance of the city centre were over. The anchor was a Quinnsworth supermarket, which also had a large hardware and 'beauty' section. In keeping with the developing trend towards evening shopping, the centre stayed open from 9.00 a.m. to 9.30 p.m. on Thursday and Friday, closing at 6.00 p.m. on the other days. As was also normal at the time, there was no Sunday opening. The swimming pool and sauna were open seven days a week.

There was no reticence about what was on offer in a large advertisement that appeared in November 1974.

What a selection! What a range! What variety! Crumlin Shopping Centre really spoils shoppers! The fairer sex particularly – they have no less than 4 exciting Boutiques, a Hairdressers, Fashion Fabrics Shop and Household Fabrics Shop to give needle negligee [*sic*] selection plus the sheer value of Quinnsworth to really bring down the cost of living. Just imagine Gaywear, Rave, Promiss and Bambinos 'n Friends Boutiques, Peter Mark Hair Salon and Wig Boutique plus Edwards and Nicholls Fabric Shops. Then you have Boylans Family Footwear and Cleggs for Shoe Repairs/leather goods. If its Knick-Knacks you're after, Hector Grey surely has it, and for the more expensive jewellery, watches and charms, Rings 'n Things have an eye-opening selection.

(Evening Herald, 7 November 1974, p. 11)

41 Crumlin shopping centre exterior. (A.J. Parker.)

42 Crumlin shopping centre interior. (A.J. Parker.)

for very many people is synonymous with Dublin, that area is O'Connell Street. This street, and the other main shopping thoroughfares, are the areas by which most people, Dubliners and visitors alike, identify our capital city in their minds' eye. This area is their yardstick for forming their opinions of Dublin. Regrettably much of this central and important area now shows visible signs of decay, of insensitive and thoughtless development and change of use, of tasteless advertising and a continuous growth of ugly plastic facades. Problems of litter, of lack of security and excessive traffic have all contributed to a degradation of the environment of this area.

It is now time for all concerned to take a hard look at what has been happening to the centre of our capital city. The area should be a showpiece of architectural sensitivity and environmental awareness but we have instead created a soulless environment which is neither attractive nor pleasant. The present condition of the city centre leads to a general attitude of carelessness and lack of concern on the part of developers, commercial interests and the public generally and a fall off in business in the area. I believe that enlightened thinking and imaginative decision making is badly needed to revive the heart of the metropolis and to make the surroundings in Dublin city centre area more pleasant for visitors and tourists, as well as for Dubliners themselves.

(Col. 653)

It was explained that Dublin Corporation had enough on their plate and this entity with a single focus and a limited time frame could achieve results quickly. Indeed, if it worked, it could be the model for infrastructural projects elsewhere. Moreover, the minister noted that the idea had been widely welcomed when it had first been mooted by the Dublin Chamber of Commerce, the Dublin City Centre Business Association and Bord Fáilte. As far back as 1978, the Dublin Chamber of Commerce had advocated the establishment of a city centre authority as an integrated solution to the problem.

Fianna Fáil opposed the setting up of the Commission and cited a number of reasons for doing so. They did not see the city centre as a problem to be solved in isolation and it made no sense to produce plans for one area that could not be integrated into an overall view of the city. Their greatest annoyance, though, was what they saw as a denial of democracy. Dublin Corporation was the body elected by the citizens of the city to manage and develop the urban area. Their prerogative was being taken from them and given to an unelected body – something Fianna Fáil themselves would later do in relation to Temple Bar. Not only that, when the life of the Commission was ended, the Corporation would have to take on the liabilities of everything that the Commission had done. In essence, the Commission was spending the Corporation's money, the money given to the Corporation by the taxpayer, without any oversight or control. Bertie Ahern took up the theme and pointed out, with some energy, that it was Dublin Corporation that developed the proposals for the improvements which the Commission was going to make. In fact, the Corporation's proposals went further, took in more streets and were altogether more comprehensive. Ahern reminded the Dáil that a similar agenda had been outlined to the Council some eighteen months prior to this legislation (Report 185/1985).

In his view, all the Corporation needed was the necessary finance, instead of which they were talking about funding a commission that would operate at the level 'of junior planning officers who decide whether a sign is legal and who sweep the streets ... We are not debating the revitalizing of the city. We are talking about where the power should lie to sweep Grafton Street and who should grow plants on O'Connell Street' (Dáil Debates (1986) vol. 369, no. 3, col. 691).

> The corporation are engaged on a number of activities designed to improve the general environment of the city centre area. One of the most important of these is the pedestrianization of streets, the special treatment of the street/pavement surfaces, the critical examination of items of street furniture and their renewal or replacement as necessary. The tasteful treatment of streets in this fashion will have a spinover [sic] effect into adjoining areas, and, it is hoped, will likely encourage owners of premises fronting on to them to take a special interest in their immediate environment and to reflect this by way of improvement in the treatment of their own frontages, sympathetic material in shop fronts and sign writing, window displays, floral displays in window boxes etc.

What emerged strongly from the contributions was that the Commission was seen as an attack on the Corporation, or more specifically a vote of no confidence in the Corporation, in which Fianna Fáil had a majority. By extension, the argument went that if they could not be trusted and given the money to undertake these lower tasks, how could they possibly be involved

105 Harbour Village in the Dún Laoghaire shopping centre. (A.J. Parker.)

106 *Pangur Bán* in the Dún Laoghaire shopping centre. (A.J. Parker.)

through the 1980s but the 'Harbour Village' idea was dropped and the space converted into nine conventional shop units. An extension was undertaken in 1991 that increased the size of the Quinnsworth operation and brought the number of retail units to 82. There was then just over 10,000 sq. m of retail space.

The end of the decade

By the end of the 1980s, it can be said that Dublin had begun to accommodate itself to the new reality that the city was polycentric and that the city centre was no longer the acme of shopping. Though the threats had been evident for many years – an increasingly suburbanized, car-loving population and a city centre that was congested and unfriendly to those cars – the city had been slow to respond. Perhaps they believed the earlier Lichfield suggestion that it was only the relative importance of the city centre that would decline and not the real, actual value of sales. Perhaps it was just the inertia that seems to have always been a feature of decision making. Certainly the two oil crises of the 1970s and the economic doldrums that characterized most of the 1980s did not help. In 1985 the City Council's planning committee met to discuss the review of the city's development plan and they reflected on the challenges that the city centre faced. The assistant city and county manager said that he 'believed that the city must be made more attractive to entice people back to shop. They must create a climate which would bring investment. There was also a need for a good transportation policy, which should include proper access to the city' (*Irish Times*, 2 October 1985, p. 6). It had a taken a long time but it seems that the city at last understood what had been going on during the previous twenty years. The discussion went on to note that there were things that traders could do such as opening for the same hours as in suburban centres, improving shopfronts and taking other measures to stimulate public interest.

The main shopping streets were more or less pedestrianized and there was the hope that Grafton Street and Henry Street might be linked via Trinity Street, Crown Alley, Merchant's Arch, the Ha'penny Bridge and Liffey Street. Multi-storey car parks were appearing, which diminished, if not removed, the pain of having to walk to the shops. The suburban shopping centre experience had been brought into the city. Initially, this needed the resources of a state company, Irish Life, but the opening of the St Stephen's Green centre saw the private sector back in the driving seat. And it was not going to stop there.

There was still plenty of derelict land, as will be explored a little further on in this text. There were plans for the land on which Jervis Street Hospital had served the city for a century or so before its incorporation into the new Beaumont Hospital. CIÉ had a large portfolio of property on the quays west of Bachelor's Walk and it was considering its options. In fact, there seemed to be so much in prospect that it could be asked whether there were going to be too many shopping centres. This was the question Parker discussed in the piece in the *Irish Times*, mentioned earlier on p. 96. He did not provide a 'yes' or 'no' answer. However, he did set out the parameters for the future. The shopper of the 1990s was going to be more sophisticated than the shopper of twenty years previously and would have definite ideas about the kind of shopping environment that would be acceptable. He suggested that 'natural light and atriums give a more pleasant feel to enclosed shopping developments; and incorporation of major design features such as waterfalls and central plazas … are necessary features to make shopping a more pleasant experience' (*Irish Times*, 12 April 1989, p. 23).

Welcome though the realization was that the city centre was in active competition with the suburbs, that competition was set to become even greater and it would be some time before it was understood that the centre had lost the battle. Tallaght was on the cusp of getting the first major element in its town centre. Dublin County Council gave planning permission for a massive shopping centre in Blanchardstown in 1987. Hardly unexpected, this was the logical consequence of the growth of the area. The City Centre Business Association objected to An Bord Pleanála on the basis that the centre would usurp the traditional role of the city centre – a view in which they were entirely correct. What was of more interest was that the City Council contemplated joining themselves to this objection. Solidarity between local governments would become a thing of the past; it would be a case of each for itself. This particular suggestion came to nothing and the City Council rejected a motion expressing 'grave concern about the impact on the city centre of the massive shopping complex proposed for Blanchardstown'. The lord mayor, Alderman Carmencita Hederman, expressed the concerns underpinning the motion when she noted that: 'the City Council had an obligation to put the interests of the city first because no one else was going to stand up for it' (*Irish Times*, 11 August 1987, p. 6). Following discussion, all shades of political opinion came together to reject the motion and support Blanchardstown.

Dublin's environment

Previous volumes in this series have not specifically focused on the quality of Dublin's urban environment. From the 1880s, Sir Charles Cameron had put in place a robust system for reporting on health issues and problems concerning food quality and supply and that continued through the decades. Other issues were not as well monitored and it was only in the 1970s, reflecting and reinforcing a greater public interest in issues that affected quality of life, that more investment was put into measuring and monitoring. However, there was one problem that Dubliners noticed.

The Liffey smells

For generations of Dubliners a walk along the quays at low tide was less than pleasurable, especially in hot weather. The smell from decaying raw sewerage was notable and it spread a considerable distance from the river. While a good system of sewers had been built as the city expanded, there was no treatment of the waste and it flowed directly into the river, relying on tidal action to move it out to sea. This, of course, was inefficient and a considerable depth of sludge built up in the river – the source of the miasma. Fish had long since deserted the river, and it had accumulated large amounts of diverse detritus, including on one occasion a piano. There was great anticipation that the problem would be solved with the opening of the impressive Mains Drainage scheme in September 1906. This had been in preparation for some time after the success of the Vartry scheme in bringing fresh water at high pressure to the city.

The Mains Drainage system involved the creation of two large interceptor sewers, north and south of the river, into which the existing system was diverted. To ensure a good flow, these had to be buried at a considerable depth; in some cases as deep as 8m. The two sewers remained independent until the northern one reached a point near Marlborough Street, from which a branch headed off to Clontarf. It was then joined to the southern flow at a point near Hawkins Street using a complex and ingenious siphon system that was buried under the Liffey and required excavations of 20m in places. From there the pipe took a fairly direct line under South Brunswick Street (Pearse Street) under Grand Canal Dock and the Dodder. It seems that the latter proved a very difficult engineering challenge. From there it eventually reached the pumping station at what had been the Pigeon House Fort. The flow was raised to ground level by pumps and then to the filtration beds where the solids were removed for disposal at sea via the SS *Shamrock* and the liquids were disinfected before being released into the Liffey. It was a primitive system by today's standards, but it served the city well until the 1990s. But did the smell go away? Not immediately!

In 1911, there was an irate letter to the *Irish Times*. In the author's view the smell on the evening of 28 July exceeded anything previously experienced, and he wrote that when 'one remembers the amount of money wasted in mains drainage schemes, it is disgraceful that such a state of affairs should exist' (*Irish Times*, 29 July 1911, p. 8). The problem did not go away and complaints about the state of the Liffey persisted into the 1930s. Dubliners still believed that sewage made its way into the river. Dublin Corporation was adamant that it did not, though it was admitted that heavy rainfall might, from time to time, cause some sewage to make its way into the Camac. However, that was both irregular and not sufficient to explain the smell.

It seemed that the explanation lay in the accumulation of mud and other debris on the bed of the river. Time and tide had not been sufficient to scour it and it remained as noxious as it was when sewage had flowed freely (*Irish Times*, 6 January 1938, p. 6). Finding an explanation was one thing, doing something about it was an entirely different matter. Once again the consequences of Dublin's fractured governance came to the fore. Responsibility for the river was divided between Dublin Corporation and the Dublin Port and Docks Board. Dublin Corporation argued that while it owned the river bed, it was the responsibility of the Port and Docks Board to 'maintain' the river. The Port and Docks Board took the view that if the river bed was the property of the Corporation, then it was they who should clean it. Nothing happened and the problem was allowed to fester, though it sometimes bubbled up (see *Irish Times*, 14 August 1943, p. 3). It was not until the 1950s that the problem was addressed. The imminence of An Tóstal caused Dublin Corporation to set about cleaning the Liffey (and the Tolka). The process took much longer than expected and in August 1954, a meeting of the Port and Docks Board considered a letter from Dublin Corporation which offered to remove the rubbish if the Port and Docks Board removed the mud and slime. The Board agreed to do what it could, without explaining what that might entail (*Irish Times*, 13 August 1954, p. 4). This led to a formal agreement of sorts in November 1954 and in the spring of 1955 a team of workmen removed all sorts of rubbish from the river from Kingsbridge to the sea. They did not remove the weed from the walls initially, however, the engineers having determined that keeping it was beneficial to maintaining the strength of the grouting between the stone blocks. This, it was suggested, would ensure that the smell remained (*Irish Times*, 26 July 1955, p. 7). The work continued through 1958 and it was claimed by the Corporation that their work, confined to the walls and the banks, was keeping the river 'comparatively clean' (*Irish Times*, 1 July 1958, p. 1). Unfortunately, though the weed was now being removed, Dubliners quickly replaced the rubbish that the Corporation had removed. Nor did the co-operation between the Corporation and the Port and Docks Board endure. In 1963, the Corporation re-iterated that it removed rubbish from time to time for health and aesthetic reasons but they had never removed mud – that, they implied was someone else's job (*Irish Times*, 27 February 1963, p. 5). The smell continued and ensured that any hot summer was also a stinking one. Letters regularly appeared in the newspapers complaining about the stench and it was the subject of comment pieces and editorials. The *Evening Herald* complained in 1964 that 'the Liffey has turned green! A dirty slimy green with refuse floating on the top from which a disgusting smell wafts over the city' (26 June 1964, p. 8). The front page of the same newspaper contained a warning from what they described as an 'eminent Dublin doctor, that the gas emanating from the Liffey would cause softening of the brain' (30 September 1967, p. 1).

The problem was twofold. The mud banks in the river were very rich in organic matter and natural decay processes produced all sorts of noxious odours. The bigger problem was that the Camac was badly polluted and it still fed into the Liffey. The Camac was a major tributary of the Liffey and flowed from the south-west from Saggart into Clondalkin and Inchicore until it met the Liffey at Heuston Station. It flowed through much of the industrialized area of the city, both old and new, and was a sewer for all sorts of pollutants, chemical and organic. Its junction point with the Liffey ensured that the entire length of the Liffey within the city centre was polluted. Moreover, changes to the channel of the Liffey, consequent on the development of the port, had diminished the scour of the tides with the result that there was a particular accumulation of material near Butt Bridge, just where everyone could smell it (*Irish Times*, 9 September 1969, p. 12). While it might be argued that stopping the pollution of the Camac in the first instance should have been the preferred solution, it seems that Dublin Corporation put its faith in the new Grand Canal drainage scheme. This scheme, part of the Greater

107 Liffey clean-up. (William Mooney, Dublin City Library and Archive.)

Dublin Drainage scheme, discussed in volume 7 (pp 204–7), was intended to meet the needs of a growing city but had proved controversial because of Dublin Corporation's initial intention to place it in the bed of the Grand Canal, a step many believed would result in the end of the canal. Public opposition ensured that the pipe would run alongside the canal on its way to Ringsend. One of the benefits of the scheme was that the wastes from the west of the city would be diverted from the Camac and thus from the Liffey. By the middle 1970s, the project was proceeding satisfactorily, if a little slower than anticipated, and it was expected that it would be complete by 1977. That left the mud banks and a final realization by Dublin Corporation that they would not disappear by themselves and that the Port and Docks Board was not going to pay to remove them. So, in 1975, they voted a sum of £25,000 to begin the work (*Irish Times*, 23 October 1975, p. 8). There are some excellent photographs in the Dublin City Photograph collection showing this process as well as reminding Dubliners that it was not a 'once and done' procedure. This was the beginning of the end of the smell though, something that had been a distinctive feature for well over a century. It was not missed!

Air quality in the city

While the Liffey smell had been a source of embarrassment and annoyance, there was never any strong evidence that it affected health. Poor air quality was a different matter. Dublin is not a particularly foggy city but its geography is suited to the formation and maintenance of fog when conditions are right. It was when fog became smog that the city faced some painful choices.

Air contains water vapour, the gaseous phase of water, the amount of which is dependent on pressure and temperature. At a given temperature and pressure, the amount of water vapour in the air is described as relative humidity, which goes from 0 per cent to 100 per cent. When relative humidity is high and pressure remains constant, a decrease in temperature will force the water vapour out of the air; it has to go somewhere and there is no longer room for it in the air molecules. This is the genesis of fogs in cities. Cities lose heat at night. During the day, the sun injects energy into the city and the various building materials store that energy. At night, this heat is radiated back into the atmosphere. If the circumstances are right, with a clear sky, there can be rapid cooling of the air close to the surface. When this air has high relative humidity, then the water vapour starts to appear out of the air as water droplets and it is these that create the fog. In essence, it is a low cloud.

There are many different types of fog but 'radiation fog' is a common urban phenomenon. This typically is experienced in autumn and early winter and occurs after dark as the air close to the surface cools. If the evening is calm, then the fog is often no more than a metre or so thick close to the surface. However, light turbulence in the air can ensure that it has greater thickness. Generally, this kind of fog does not persist for long – a few hours usually – but there are circumstances in which it can last.

This is when a temperature inversion occurs above a city. Warmer air rises and cools. Normally, there is a steady decrease in the temperature of the air as height increases. However, sometimes, the cooling of the air at lower levels is more marked and colder air meets a layer of warmer air at higher elevations. This layer of colder air cannot penetrate the warmer air; effectively a lid is put on the rising air.

So radiation fog can develop below the inversion layer and the turbulence caused by air continuing to rise ensures that fog can attain a considerable depth. Normally this would clear quickly but where a city is contained within a bowl or with a shield of mountains, then the stability this provides can ensure that the inversion will persist for a much longer period. Although

Dublin's mountains are not particularly high, their location to the south and west of the city causes them to act as a shield from the prevailing winds from the south-west. This can facilitate the type of conditions in which an inversion can occur and extend the duration of the resulting radiation fog.

It seems that Dublin experienced serious fogs from time to time from the nineteenth century onwards. Interestingly, these appear not to have been particularly newsworthy for the Dublin newspapers and they get scant mention. It was often left to the regional newspapers to record the event.

Dense fog was reported on the night 23 January 1872 during the early part of the night. However, it made the news only because three deaths occurred during the event. Captain William Hern of the brig *Eden* was found drowned in Custom House Dock following, it was alleged, an altercation with the mate on the schooner *Alicia*, which was moored nearby. A man fell into the Liffey near the Custom House at about 8.00 p.m. and drowned. The third death was of a man who drove his carriage and horse into the Grand Canal between Mount Street and Grand Canal bridges. The horse and carriage were retrieved but the driver was drowned (*Irish Times*, 23 January 1872, p. 3). A November night in 1906 was described in the *Cork County Eagle* (10 November 1906, p. 1). It reported that dense fog descended on Dublin city and such was its intensity that people could not find footpaths and bumped into each other and cyclists were forced to dismount. Visibility was down to three or four yards and drivers of trams and drays found it difficult to avoid collisions. It was noted that in suburban areas, the street lighting failed to penetrate the gloom. It fits well the description of radiation fog, appearing just after sunset on a Tuesday evening in November and beginning to dissipate by about 11.00 p.m. that night. It was noted that by midnight that things were once again normal.

Fogs can also occur in the morning, if the air temperature has fallen sufficiently during the night, and a noteworthy fog was reported in the *Liberator* for January 1924 (8 January 1924, p. 4). It was noted that it was the heaviest for years and persisted well into the morning and required that same level of lighting as for the evening. An unusual spell of cold weather in 1935 resulted in dense early morning fogs, which delayed ferry crossings. The weather was colder than it had been in the previous twenty years and it was reported in the *Strabane Chronicle* (28 December 1935, p. 2) that the River Tolka had frozen and that there had been severe disruption to transport and deliveries because of the frozen roads. Similarly cold weather (*Sunday Independent*, 19 December 1937, p. 14) produced dense fog with the result that

DUBLIN'S HEALTHIEST AND LOVELIEST SUBURB
one mile from sea
MOUNT MERRION PARK
STILLORGAN ROAD

★ MOUNTAIN AND SEA AIR
★ 350 ft. ABOVE SEA LEVEL
★ FREE FROM FOG

LABOUR-SAVING HOUSES from £950

OPEN DAILY, Sundays Included, From 12 noon to 10 p.m.

REASONABLE DEPOSIT ACCEPTED AND EASY TERM PAYMENTS FOR BALANCE

SHOPS,
CHURCHES AND
SCHOOLS
ON THE
ESTATE.

EXCELLENT
'BUS SERVICE
Nos.
63, 46,
46a and 84.

The Decorations and finish of these Beautiful Homes
cannot be excelled

Visit the 1939 Exhibition House
FREE LEASES

SOLICITORS—WHITE & MEARES,   ARCHITECTS—MILLAR & SYMES.   BUILDERS—JOHN KENNY & SONS, LTD.
11 St. Stephen's Green, Dublin.   39 Kildare Street, Dublin.   Harcourt Road, Dublin.

TO
IRISH HOMES LTD.

Telephone: Dublin 61946-7 and Blackrock 344.

108 Absence of fog as a selling point in Mount Merrion, 1939.
(*Sunday Independent*, 6 August 1939.)

visibility in Drumcondra at 7.00 p.m. was no more than 20 yards (which does not seem all that bad!).

Saturday, 13 January 1940 saw what was described as the 'worst fog for a quarter of a century' (*Sunday Independent*, 14 January 1940, p. 7). It was described as being so dangerous between 7.00 p.m. and 9.00 p.m. that several cross-city bus routes had to be stopped. The fog spread out into the suburbs and it was said that only pedestrians could get about. As was usual, the fog began to thin between 9.00 p.m. and 10.00 p.m. and by 11.00 p.m. the sky was clear.

However, as the fog cleared, pedestrians were treated to the unusual sight of bus conductors walking in front of their buses checking that the route was clear.

The *Sunday Independent* reported in November 1945 that two people had drowned in the Grand Canal on the previous night in two separate incidents. In one case, it seemed that a cyclist had become disoriented at Parnell Bridge and had wandered into the canal (25 November 1945, p. 1). Fog was also front-page news on 22 March 1953 when the *Sunday Independent* recounted that it had caused disruption during the previous night and into the early morning. It was worst in suburban areas early in the night, with the central areas largely unaffected, but it spread to all areas by midnight. The worst affected locations included Clontarf, Dollymount, Donnybrook, Stillorgan Road, Dolphin's Barn and Dún Laoghaire. It caused buses to pull over and wait until the air cleared, and ferry services were delayed. Dublin Airport had been forced to close on the previous day but was not affected by this episode.

These various reports suggest that fog was a common occurrence in Dublin and that even disruptive episodes were not seen as particularly newsworthy. It cannot be that disruptive fogs occurred only on a Saturday night so that they might be reported in the *Sunday Independent*. It seems more reasonable to suggest that it was newsworthy only in the context of a Sunday newspaper. That it was a relatively common occurrence is supported by an advertisement for houses in Mount Merrion in 1939. At this time, Irish Homes were building their suburb, which was distinctive for the quality of design, the variety in house types on offer and because facilities such as shopping were included in development. Among the pleasing aspects advertised in 1939 (*Sunday Independent*, 6 August 1939, p. 4) was the healthy sea and mountain air that resulted from being 350 feet above sea level, and the freedom from fog.

A study of the occurrence of non-frontal fog or mist at Dublin Airport in 1948 looked at the data for the period 1939–47. Taking a very broad definition of what constituted a fog or mist, the following number of instances were reported.

October	25
November	36
December	27
January	25
February	12

A total of 46 instances were attributed to radiation fog and it was found that most cases had dispersed before noon and that in only two cases had it persisted during the afternoon (Timoney, 1949).

Fogs may have been regular but they seemed to have been more of a nuisance than a real problem, probably because they do not seem to have been heavily polluted. Air quality did not figure in the annual Corporation reports on the state of public health, which were comprehensive in many ways. Dublin did not develop heavy industry, and therefore did not suffer the intense industrial pollution that was the lot of many cities. In Dublin, in the nineteenth century, domestic fires would have been the major source of smoke but many of the poor in the more densely occupied parts of the city would scarcely have been able to afford coal. By the end of the nineteenth century London was infamous for its 'pea-souper' fogs, which reduced visibility to feet and turned air toxic.

Though Dublin had its fogs in the 1950s, these were as nothing compared to the fog London experienced between 5 and 9 December 1952. The weather pattern was typical in that an anticyclone with little wind settled over the city, creating an inversion. This trapped a dense layer of airborne pollutants, mainly arising from the use of coal, over the city. In the post-war period, the quality of coal was often poor, with large amounts of sulphur released in its burning. On the first day, the impact was felt most around Westminster but it soon spread in all directions and covered an area from the North Downs to the Chilterns of at least 20km to 30km along the Thames Valley. While the intensity varied during the event visibility was less than 20m over much of central London north of the Thames. It was all-pervasive for five days but dispersed very quickly once the weather changed. However, the impact was huge, with estimates of between 4,000 and 10,000 deaths directly from the pollution and perhaps 100,000 suffering ill effects (Wilkins, 1954). These conditions were commonplace in heavily polluted districts such as the Potteries in Staffordshire. It was not for nothing that it was called 'the Black Country' and it was not uncommon for all sight of the sun to be obscured for days by the smoke coming from the numerous kilns in the area. This is captured wonderfully by William Blake's photographs from the 1910s onwards and nothing had changed much by the 1950s. The fact that such had happened in London, though, was instrumental in the passing of the various Clean Air Acts over the next few years.

Dublin had been spared that but its time was coming. The conditions that produce significant fogs will also ensure that airborne pollutants will not escape lower levels in the city. There is no essential difference between 'fog' and 'smog'. Urban air has contained pollutants for as long as cities were centres of production and for as long as residents lit fires. The term 'smog' came into general usage in the early part of the twentieth century to describe the phenomenon of smoky fogs, the heavily polluted fogs that assailed many cities in the industrialized west. Just as the water vapour has nowhere to go in 'foggy' conditions, so too the smoke is trapped. As car usage increased, especially in the United States, it became common to differentiate what occurred in summer (summer smog) from the more usual 'winter smog'. The former, photochemical smog, was the result of sunlight reacting with nitrogen oxides and volatile oxides in the atmosphere, which leaves airborne particles and creates ozone pollution at lower levels. Other noxious compounds may well be present and acid rain from nitric and sulphuric acids may result at some distance from the city. Motor vehicles are a hugely important source of these pollutants but so are a variety of industrial processes. The materials necessary to produce this kind of smog are present in many cities but sunlight is necessary to drive the chemical reactions and so smogs of this kind are associated more with cities in warmer climates.

Smog became more and more of an issue in Dublin as the city grew and a larger population was contained within the semi-bowl of the city. Car ownership grew too from the 1960s onwards but Dublin was fortunate in that it never experienced the temperatures necessary to generate significant photochemical smogs. Nonetheless cars were certainly adding to the pollution burden of the city and a trip to the Wicklow Mountains would reveal a layer of hazy pollution over the city that seemed to persist no matter what the weather. The bigger problem was coal. The population of the city was becoming more and more accustomed to using private cars and they were also becoming accustomed to central heating. From the 1960s, it increasingly became a feature of new housing, though mainly in the private sector initially. For unfathomable reasons, it became common to decide that the ideal temperature for a house was in excess of 22°C, temperatures rarely experienced outside even on the warmest summer days. There were three methods of central heating available. In the first system, radiators were heated by circulating water heated by a boiler that operated on gas, oil or solid fuel. More expensive houses might have a hot-air system whereby warmed air was pumped around the house having been heated by electricity or by an oil- or gas-based system. There was a third option in having under-floor electric heating or by using storage heaters in which off-peak electricity was used to heat brick-like containers that later radiated the heat. Electricity was cheap and there did not seem to be much difference in the running costs of the various options at the beginning of the 1970s. Builders were sufficiently confident in the future of central heating

7 reasons why you should specify ELECTRICAIRE*

the warm-air ducted heating system
that's clean, economical and trouble-free

1   **SUITABLE FOR NEW HOUSING:**
    Because there are no chimney flues or bulky storage containers to
    contend with, Electricaire is ideal for building into new houses.
    Fire-places may be eliminated, reducing construction costs.

2   **LOW INSTALLATION COST:**
    The system is easy to install: the cost of installation is very reason-
    able and compares very favourably with most other systems.

3   **RUNNING COSTS:**
    Running costs are highly competitive with other fuels.

4   **FREE DESIGN:**
    The design of Electricaire installations is carried out by specialists
    who supervise the actual installation work as it progresses; this
    service is completely free.

5   **FREE ADVISORY SERVICE:**
    At the first installation a representative of the Board is present to
    help and advise.

6   **PACKAGED DEAL:**
    The heater, plenum chamber, ducting and all necessary equipment
    for the installation is supplied as a 'package deal' by the E.S.B.

7   **FREE COMMISSIONING:**
    The commissioning of each installation is carried out by the Board
    free of charge.

**Electricaire is a clean-heat system
and causes no pollution of any kind.**

For further information please contact
**DOMESTIC DEVELOPMENT SECTION
ESB Lower Fitzwilliam Street, Dublin 2**

109 Advertisement for Electricaire, 1972.
(*Irish Press*, 11 March 1972, p. 16.)

that houses were built without fireplaces or chimneys. One such example was
Claremont Court in Glasnevin, across the road from the cemetery. The houses
were innovative in design with quite high density (for the times) and open
plan gardens. They offered four bedrooms, separate sitting and dining rooms
plus what Healy Homes described as an economical and efficient Electricaire
central heating system (*Irish Times*, 20 July 1973, p. 24). This allowed them
to be built without chimneys, though they did have fireplaces. A piece in

the *Irish Times* emphasized the virtues of heating by electricity. Under the heading 'Heating by electricity is cheap clean and efficient' it extolled the virtues of electricity, not the least of which was that it was very clean and completely odourless. This also made a significant contribution to the drive for clean air. However, unwittingly, the article foretold the future in that 'all the features would be irrelevant if the cost of running the Electricaire system was prohibitive but, in fact, Electricaire running costs compare favourably with other systems' (*Irish Times*, 18 September 1972, p. 17). By 1972, it was rare for new houses to be advertised without central heating. Courtlands was a new development of four-bedroomed semi-detached houses off Griffith Avenue in north Dublin. As well as the usual amenities, it offered 'a spacious lounge, separate dining room, fitted kitchen, garage and walk-in cloakroom'. It had oil-fired central heating throughout and radiators in each room (*Irish Independent*, 12 May 1972, p. 22).

The 1970s proved to be a period of recession and high inflation with wages chasing inflation and prices. The Yom Kippur War of October 1973 may have produced a useful military stalemate in the Middle East but it is credited with precipitating the oil crisis of that year as the Organization of the Petroleum Exporting Countries (OPEC) imposed an oil embargo on those countries it believed to have supported Israel. The resulting shortages had short- and long-term effects on the world economy, not the least of which was the realization by the oil producers that they could control price. The price of oil quadrupled in the period to March 1974 when the embargo was lifted. A second oil crisis followed the Iranian Revolution in 1979. Though this affected only about 4 per cent of global supplies, it resulted in a doubling of crude oil prices by the following year. The 1980s and into the 1990s saw the price of oil decline but there was no return to a world of cheap electricity.

Ireland generated 55.7 per cent of its electricity from oil or coal in 1971. By 1980, this had been reduced to 37 per cent, largely through the substitution of gas, but the amount of electricity produced had increased by 82 per cent. Dublin was hugely important in electricity production: 23.3 per cent of output was generated on the Ringsend 'peninsula' in 1970 and 30.8 per cent in 1980. Production by then had shifted from the Ringsend Power Station to the Poolbeg Power Station, with its now familiar twin chimneys.

The price of both heating oil and electricity rose dramatically and changed the dynamic in home heating. Between 1968 and 1980, consumer prices more than quintupled; just between 1975 and 1980, they almost doubled. However, the prices of light and fuel had risen far more than prices in any other economic

110 The ESB Poolbeg peninsula.

sector. From 1968 to 1980, they had risen by over six and a half times; from 1975 to 1980, by two and a half times. The price of a single unit of electricity was 0.892p in 1970 but was 3.5p in 1980. It was not just prices – supply of electricity had proven to be an issue too.

Oil-fired heating and electric central heating especially were now both uncompetitive and uncertain. A comparison was offered in the *Irish Times* in 1980. An article by Frank McDonald discussed the virtues of district heating schemes and provided the following estimates of annual costs for an average household from Peter Byrne, chairman of the Energy Conservation and District Heating Association.

District heating	£215
Oil	£350
Peat	£252
High-grade coal	£274
Electric storage	£465
Town gas	£695

The switch to solid-fuel heating was supported by government policy, which sought to reduce the country's dependence on imported oil. Advertisements

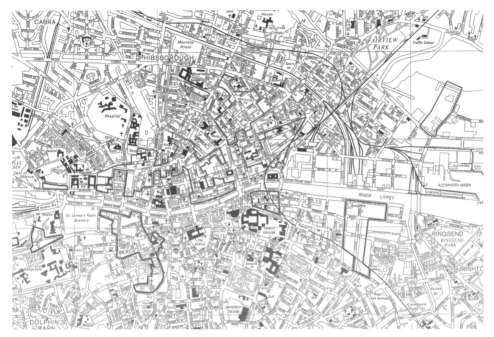

132 Designated areas, 1994.

incentive zone was reduced from 530 to 300 acres (SI 407/1994). The pump
had already been primed enough along the quays, with the exception of
Bachelor's Walk and Usher's Quay, where development continued, while
Gardiner Street middle was largely rebuilt. The areas included were:

- George's Quay and Pearse Street;
- Eccles Street;
- Gardiner Street Lower/Amiens Street area;
- Gardiner Street Upper/Mountjoy Square;
- Parkgate Street area;
- Benburb Street area;
- Thomas Street/Francis Street;
- Grand Canal Docks; and
- East Wall.

(SI 407/1994)

The zones were much more fragmented than previously and zigzagged over
their area reflecting what must have been a tortuous decision-making process.
The inclusion of parts of Benburb Street, once again, showed just how difficult

133 The 'favoured' side of Francis Street, 1987.

it was to get comprehensive redevelopment. The newly designated areas focused on the north city; why anyone felt that regeneration might happen there without such incentives is astonishing. Included or extended were stretches from the Custom House to the North Circular Road. The inclusion of the Jervis Street area was, at last, a recognition that the prime shopping district was quite limited in the north city and did not extend much to the west of Liffey Street. The zone around Smithfield was extended to include the Hardwicke, Whitworth and Richmond Hospital campuses, which, though containing some fine buildings, had struggled to find new roles. Recognizing the lack of spill-over, the west side of Francis Street was designated, as was part of Watling Street and a zone to the south of Usher's Island. It would have been better to have designated the entire Liberties area as this location continued to experience difficulties which persist to the present day. It can be summed up by saying that the incentive area encompassed much of the north side and very little of the south city except for the Liberties and George's Quay. The CHDDA/DDA and Temple Bar Properties were managing their own renewal programmes by this time.

Two outlying areas were also included. One was on the south bank of the Tolka, north of East Wall Road. This was destined to become Eastpoint, home to many of the technology companies and their satellites. It is probably unknown to most Dubliners as there is no through traffic and it is not visible from the road, except to those walking in Clontarf. The other outlier was destined to become much more visible and, in many respects, a metaphor for the new Dublin. This was the first designation of the Grand Canal Docks area, the area the *Irish Times* felt would spontaneously develop. It has now become spectacularly successful as a middle-class, multi-cultural, multi-lingual enclave in the city.

An interesting feature of this scheme was the designation of individual streets to provide encouragement for refurbishment for residential use of the upper floors of business premises in Capel Street, Meath Street, Thomas Street and South Great George's Street. Meath Street and Thomas Street had long since lost their roles as major retail streets and had settled into local provision. Capel Street too had slipped in importance over the decades and was perhaps no more than a tertiary street, but the inclusion of South Great George's Street showed how far this street had fallen.

The docklands

The renewal of the Custom House Docks area began with the passing of the Urban Renewal Act 1986. While the original Gregory concept of public ownership did not come to pass, its special character was recognized by the creation of a development authority to oversee its regeneration. Nobody, however, could have realized just how significant this authority would become in the reimagining and redesign of a large portion of the city. Moore's volume (2008) in this series has analysed this process in detail so only a short reworking of the material is presented here.

The Custom House Docks Development Authority (CHDDA) was formally established on 17 November 1986. It was a small body of only six people and in its Custom House Docks Planning Scheme, which was published in 1987, it claimed that this was the first 'instance of a formalized comprehensive development partnership between public and private sectors in Ireland – a partnership in which Government incentives provide the catalyst to encourage private enterprise' (p. 3). Perhaps the combination of descriptors above made it unique but the Wide Streets Commission has to have a claim to primacy while the reserved-area housing policy operated in a very similar way. Likewise, the claim that the site was the 'the single largest block of prime urban land to be designated for redevelopment this century' depends on what

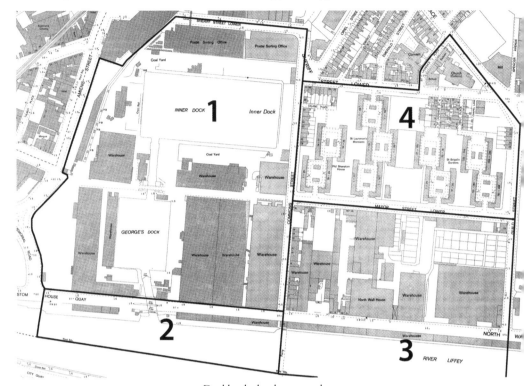

134 Docklands development phases.
(Ordnance Survey plan, 1, 1:1000, Sheets 3264-1 and 3264-2, 1972.)

is understood by 'prime urban land'. Despite the attempts at puffery, this was
a very significant development opportunity and dependent on the incentives
being attractive enough to interest the commercial sector. The 11ha site had
the advantage that it was not too deep into the docklands and had good river
frontage. It was within walking distance of O'Connell Bridge and all of the
city-centre facilities.

Development in the area enjoyed a substantial range of incentives available
under the Urban Renewal Act 1986 as well as those set out in the Finance Act
1986. However, it was to be an element in the Finance Act 1987 which was to
prove both controversial and crucial. This provided that there would be a 10
per cent rate of corporation tax to international financial services and ancillary
services associated with such services that located in the Custom House Docks
area.

Though a large plot, it was a relatively small part of the docklands, bounded
by the quays, Commons Street, Sheriff Street Lower and Amiens Street. There

184 The completed development of Ha'penny Bridge House, 1994.

rooms appear in *Ulysses*. It had survived quite well up to the early 1970s as figures 185 and 186 show. By the 1980s decay had set in. A person taking a walk from Liffey Street towards O'Connell Street in 1983 would have passed four demolished buildings, a large motorcycle salesroom, a large warehousing and commercial transport hub for CIÉ, a couple of antique shops, and a second-hand clothes shop with two vacant units on either side. Murph's restaurant stood in splendid isolation with two derelict units on one side and a vacant building on the other. Moving on, the walker would have passed Carroll's house furnishers, a club, a tailor and an estate agent until coming to the Bachelor Inn, the well-known public house at the corner with Bachelor's Way.

The decay of this stretch was driven by commercial speculation, which had been going on since the 1970s but which had accelerated during the 1980s. CIÉ bore a heavy responsibility for this because it still had hopes of being able to develop its long-awaited and greatly needed central bus station. They had got as far as having outline plans prepared for both sides of the river in the middle 1970s (see earlier discussion) but nothing had come of this. They still had hopes for an impressive development on the left bank of the river, after all Dublin Corporation had endorsed the need for redevelopment here and

185 Bachelor's Walk in the late 1960s.

186 Bachelor's Walk at the O'Connell Street end in 1974.

was anxious to join up the two shopping districts in the city. The dereliction east of Liffey Street was caused by property speculation, which began in the 1970s but reached a peak in the middle 1980s. By then, the developer Tom Gilmartin had plans for a massive shopping centre and he involved Arlington Securities, a UK company. CIÉ became involved and the scheme became one for a shopping centre on a large 3.5 acre (1.4ha) site, with a bus station on top, eliminating the existing minor streets. This was bound to be controversial since some original Georgian houses would be demolished. Site acquisition was another issue. By the end of the 1980s, they had only 40 per cent or so of the site and it now seemed that Dublin Corporation was not going to help them with compulsory purchase. Additionally, it seemed that CIÉ would not get EC help with the project. Had the proposal been live during the 1960s, the planning response would have been different for reasons already explored here, but the money might have been just as elusive. This development proposal fizzled out for reasons that were explored at the Mahon Tribunal in 2004. The area continued to deteriorate, assisted by a number of mysterious fires – one in February 1990 and another in August of that year – which resulted in serious damage to no. 7 and the destruction of no. 8 – the Georgian buildings of concern (see *Irish Times*, 21 August 1990, p. 9 for an excellent summary of what happened to the site). Arlington decided to get rid of their holdings and they were put up for sale on 8 October 1990. The sale involved six separate lots, three encompassing most of Bachelor's Walk, bounded by North Lotts, with the others involving more discrete blocks on Middle Abbey Street (see *Irish Times*, 21 August 1990, p. 9).

The now ubiquitous Zoe Developments bought the sites from Litton Lane to Liffey Street, bounded by The Lotts and sought planning permission in April 1993. They intended to build 395 apartments with 1,321 sq. m of retail development in three-, four-, five- and six-storey blocks on the site. There would be 177 car-parking spaces, with some underground and others at ground level, with access via the Lotts. The plan envisaged the demolition of nos. 8–12 inclusive, the CIÉ building, but it was intended to retain and refurbish no. 7, one of the earliest Georgian houses in the city, which had excellent interiors. The large remaining lot on Bachelor's Walk became a hotel, built by the same developers as Clifden Court. Planning permission was granted for the 126-bedroom Arlington Hotel in June 1996. It was also the middle 1990s before there was much interest in developing the sites available on Middle Abbey Street. Despite is proximity to O'Connell Street, it was never a major retail hub and was home to a variety of commercial offices,

187 A view of Bachelor's Walk in 1990, following the CIÉ fire.

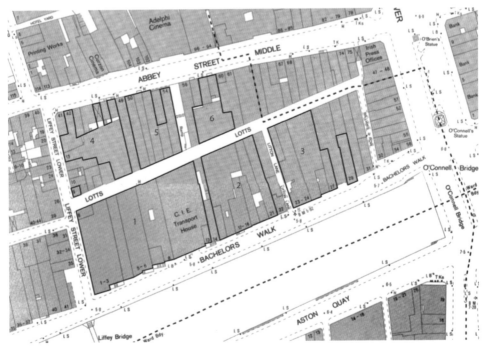

188 The development opportunity in 1990.

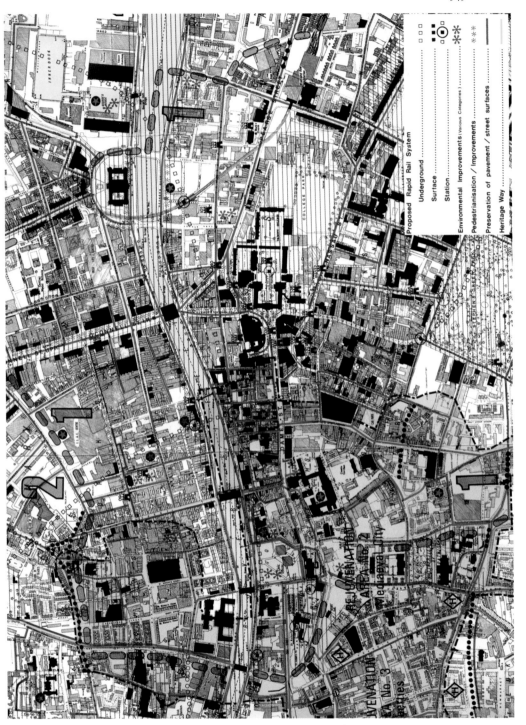

227 Dublin City Development Plan 1991. Extract from Map 6B.

and Dún Laoghaire managed to produce a further variation in September 1983. In that month, it went on public display in Dún Laoghaire and then went on tour to Blackrock Town Hall and Dalkey Town Hall. Unlike the county, Dún Laoghaire did not get embroiled in land zoning or re-zoning; it had very little land left for development. Its boundaries had not been altered since 1930, despite considerable expansion to the west and it would have to wait until the local government reforms of the 1980s and 1990s to be united with its suburbs. The 1983 draft plan also ended any love affair with the motor car. Unlike the first plans, the proposals for road widening were more modest and no motorways were accommodated. The biggest change was the dramatic increase in protected structures and views. A total of 19 views and 52 forest and woodland locations were given protection. Their 'List A' now contained 160 structures compared to under 20 previously and, all in all, over 1,100 elements were given some level of protection. It was all too late to save Frascati House in Blackrock but a welcome development to many. Also welcomed was the presentation of the document, which was said to be a much more coherent statement of policy than the previous one which was described as an incoherent series of lists.

Matters were more exciting in Dublin County because this is where the expansion of Dublin was going to happen and this involved the transformation of agricultural land into development land. The revised plan was not adopted until 1983 by which time the entire process had become mired in controversy. It is beyond the scope of this book to explore the details of the controversial land zonings and rezonings. However, it is illustrative of the issue that in 1983 it was reported that the Council made more use of Section 4 motions than any other. As noted above, Section 4 motions were intended to be rare and exceptional but in Dublin County Council they became a standard device to obtain planning permission and to alter the development plan. In reply to a question from Councillor Eithne FitzGerald, the county manager revealed that over the previous two years that twelve Section 4 planning permissions and 27 'material contraventions of the development plan' permissions had been granted by the Council (*Irish Times*, 5 June 1983, p. 4). This put the Council third only to Galway and Mayo. It was said that so many motions appeared on the Council agenda that it was impossible to conduct ordinary business because such motions took precedence over everything else. The *Irish Times* returned to the topic on 17 October 1983 (p. 6) and this produced a furious response from Dublin County councillors. The mood of the meeting may be gauged from the reported comments of Myles Tierney, who stated:

I, therefore, ask you chairman to seek an immediate meeting with the Editor of *The Irish Times* in order to allow him an opportunity to show why his representatives should not be excluded from reporting the proceedings of this council in view of the defamatory, politically biased, selective, propagandistic and generally untrue, unjust and unfair report of Monday, October 17th. I further ask you to request the Organisation and Procedures Committee to consider whether or not the representatives of *The Irish Times* should not be excluded from attending at all meetings of the council pending a satisfactory resolution of the matters raised by me.

(*Irish Times,* 22 October 1983, p. 7)

This environment was hardly conducive to producing a good development plan.

Changes to governance

The Local Government (Reorganisation) Act of 1985 finally started the long-awaited reform of local government in Dublin. The growth of Dublin had always had peculiar characteristics which resulted from the development of independent suburbs in the nineteenth century, the townships. Many of these had been absorbed into the city by the end of 1930, though the coastal townships retained their independence as Dún Laoghaire. Howth was also independent, a circumstance that was of significant relevance to late-night drinkers seeking to exploit the 'bona fide' rule. There was a further attempt to produce a more coherent city structure in the report of the Local Government (Dublin) Tribunal, which began its work late in 1935 and published its report in 1938. It was an excellent report, which suggested a multi-level system of governance. Perhaps it was its radical nature that ensured that it was ignored. The last meeting of Howth's Urban District Council was held on 11 August 1942. This was two years after the passing of the Local Government (Amendment) Act of 1940 which provided for Howth's absorption into the city and which turned out to be the most tangible manifestation of the tribunal's report. After that, little happened and some minor boundary changes were the only significant alterations to the governance structure.

There was an attempt in the early 1970s by the Fianna Fáil government to introduce a reorganization of local government. A white paper was published on 11 February 1971 that proposed concentrating local administration into a much smaller number of county councils. This would involve the abolition of 28 town commissioners and 55 borough and urban district councils, and not all current county councils would survive since it was envisaged that some could have jurisdiction over more than one county. The driving force was the cost of public administration and it was believed that significant savings could be obtained. For Dublin, this meant the absorption of Dublin Corporation and Dún Laoghaire Borough into the County Council, meaning that the entire county of Dublin would henceforth be administered by a high-level regional council. This must have produced a wry smile from John Garvin, the Dublin city commissioner. Dublin Corporation had been abolished in April 1969 for a failure to strike a rate and the city was now governed by a single commissioner (and not three as had happened in the 1920s). John Garvin had been the secretary to the 1938 tribunal and now, at the end of a distinguished career in public service, he might at last see at least one of the recommendations of 'his' report implemented. Reaction to the proposals was swift and not enthusiastic. The deputy chairman of Dublin County Council, Senator John Boland, was quoted as saying that the proposals would put more power in the hands of the bureaucrats and 'and the ordinary man in the street would have less say in local affairs' (*Irish Independent*, 12 February 1971, p. 3).

What made this plan distinctive was that only one layer was proposed, though at the same time it was recognized that there might be a need for some level of activity at higher- and lower-level tiers. The county was chosen as the fundamental layer because of its high recognition factor. It was understood that boundaries were not always coherent and that some counties were simply not big enough to produce the efficiencies being sought, but no counties were specified for administrative amalgamation. The proposals were somewhat vague with regard to other tiers. The regional dimension was recognized and it was understood that there might be a need for regional structures. At a lower level there might be area committees, comprised of representatives of local and community interests as well as elected members. These would provide a local 'voice' and 'preserve the sense of involvement of the citizens' though without any statutory power it was left unclear how effective such committees might be.

The proposals in relation to Dublin were quite opaque. It was argued that the best way to proceed was for all local services to be offered by a unitary authority. At the same time, it was recognized that there could be a distinction between 'common services' and 'local services'; the latter might reflect the needs of rural parts of the county. These services might be managed by a local committee but if there was such a committee, then it would make sense for it to have its own staff and premises so that as many public services could be provided as possible. It seemed a rather decentralized centralized system!

The government envisaged delegating as many functions as appropriate, without specifying what these might be. They were clear though that they did not intend on relinquishing control over borrowing and in the absence of provision for local taxation, this ensured that any local autonomy would be severely limited.

Reaction within Dublin Corporation was muted given the lack of a platform for the elected representatives, so the focus shifted to the county. The county councillors rejected the proposals at a meeting in May 1971, with even the Fianna Fáil councillors being opposed (*Irish Times*, 6 May 1971, p. 5). One interesting objection was that it was realized that it would be very difficult to get elected to such a large body.

Once the period of consultation concluded, the minister declared that he was not persuaded by the objections and would press ahead with the reorganization of Dublin. This would happen after the local elections (postponed for a year to 1973) took place (*Irish Times*, 27 October 1972, p. 1).

Ireland joined the EEC on 1 January 1973 and there was a change of government following a general election on 28 February. One consequence was that the minister for local government, Mr Tully, decided not to proceed with the process of local-government reorganization as set out in the white paper, and the matter was dropped, much to the relief of many in local government. There was a promise to revisit the issue in the future but the minister indicated that it was not a matter that required urgent attention (*Irish Times*, 4 April 1973, p. 1). Another outcome of the general election was a further postponement of the local elections. The minister came up with a creative solution to the continuing proroguing of Dublin Corporation by appointing the elected councillors as commissioners until the elections took place in June 1974. This resulted in the newly appointed commissioners having their first meeting on 7 May 1973 (*Irish Times*, 5 May 1973, p. 13).

It took a while before the matter was reconsidered, so the reform process that was initiated in 1985 had been long awaited and was generally welcomed. The second-stage debate on the Local Government Reorganisation Bill took place on 14 March 1985, with the minister for the environment, Mr Kavanagh, explaining that this bill was one of a number that would bring reform to local government. Among the promised reforms was the devolution of power from central government together with a new system of funding.

This particular piece of legislation dealt with the reorganization of the governance structure and the creation of new councils. Or at least, it was a step in that direction because the immediate purpose of the legislation was to sort out electoral areas for the forthcoming local elections. Therefore even though there was a nod towards the need for more coherent governance in the debate, the main interest was electoral. This resulted in little being said about the benefits that the new structure would bring, or about the deliberative process that had led to the outcome that was being discussed. What the minister outlined was not particularly innovative and bore more than a passing resemblance to a dusted-down version of the 1938 report. He explained that consideration had been given to a single authority for the metropolitan area but that this had been rejected on the basis that the city was too complex and such an authority would be too far removed from the people. With much greater granularity, they considered setting up a number of local councils, each serving a population of 100,000 people or so. These would be responsible for the normal local-government functions in their areas. This was rejected because there would be an inevitable problem of co-ordination or the lack of it. In fact, an overarching directly elected metropolitan council would be needed. He did not explain why this metropolitan council would have to be directly elected but he did not need to; this was not going to be an option. A related option was the reduction of the size of the city to something approaching the inner city, with the remainder governed by a number of councils. Again, this was rejected because it would sunder people from the entity that they had grown to know (and love?). This was surely somewhat of a 'straw man' since the proposal did not solve any problem that had been identified.

Instead the government had decided on a system of four councils for the entire Dublin county area. The boundaries were decided by geography. The Liffey provided the boundary between the north and south councils, except for a piece of Lucan which was added to the northern area for reasons of administrative convenience. The Dodder was the dividing line between a west and east council. Well, in fact, it was a bit more complicated than that and the minister explained that it would

> proceed from the Dodder, and the city boundary, at Woodside Drive, by the boundaries of the Castle Golf Club and of Marley Park, to Rockbrook and then by the Pine Forest Road to Glendoo Mountain and the junction with the Wicklow county boundary. This line follows townland boundaries or other natural or physical features which facilitate the north/south direction of the division.

These divisions produced the new councils of Dún Laoghaire-Rathdown, Dublin-Belgard, Dublin-Fingal and, of course, the existing county borough with some small boundary changes. It was still Dublin Corporation, though also known as Dublin City Council, and would remain so until the Local Government Act 2001 abolished the old county borough system and the revised entity decided to call itself Dublin City Council, thus erasing nearly 1,000 years of history.

The minister recognized that having four councils did not solve the problem of co-ordination and announced that a further piece of legislation would result in the establishment of metropolitan council to be 'nominated by the four mainline authorities to consider matters of overall interest and to act as a co-ordinating influence in relation to services and programmes that will require to be approached on a metropolitan basis'. This was more than a little vague but the key element was that it would be a body nominated from the elected councils.

And that was that! Other than outlining other options and then rejecting them there was little justification as to why four councils was the best option available or why two were needed south of the Liffey but only one to the north. This was the most important change in governance (or was going to be at some point in the future) in over a century but it seemed to be taken rather casually by all involved. Fianna Fáil's response, delivered by Bobby Molloy TD, called attention to this. As he put it: 'The Bill before the House cannot by any stretch of the imagination be considered as implementing major reforms of the local government system. It deals solely with electoral matters and makes no reference to the functions carried out by local authorities.' However, then he went on to spend most of his time speaking about the electoral issues that arose.

Nothing of consequence happened following the enactment of the legislation. The local elections took place and the census of population duly reported its results on the basis of the new electoral areas. In 1991, the next steps were taken, with the enactment of the Local Government Act 1991. This began the practical process of reorganizing the county into the four new councils, with the new ones named Fingal, South Dublin and Dún Laoghaire-Rathdown. Specifically, Dublin County Council was required to establish what was called an 'area committee' for each of the new council areas and to give them responsibility for a variety of functions. This, in essence, was permitting the new structure to work, to some degree, under the umbrella of the County Council. One of the tasks given to the managers of these areas, together with

Dublin Corporation, was to prepare a 'reorganization report', which would set out the practical steps needed to allow the new councils to operate. This was supplied to the minister and duly published in July 1992. Unsurprisingly, this recommended that the councils would operate independently and autonomously, providing their own services with only sewage, waste and water production being provided on a wider Dublin basis. This was a missed opportunity to ensure an enhanced level of metropolitan service delivery, but organizations tend to be loath to cede any control, especially to a potential overlord.

These provisions were given legislative effect in the local government (Dublin) bill, 1993, whose second stage was introduced in the Dáil on Wednesday 3 November 1993 by Michael Smith, minister for the environment. The maintenance of local autonomy made the establishment of the over-arching regional council all the more important. Regional councils were provided for in the Planning Act 1991 and the minister indicated that he intended to create one for Dublin. Clause 43 of the 1991 act provided, inter alia, for 'the conferral of functions on the authority in relation to the coordination of the provision of public services or specified public services in the region of the authority'. However the words used by the minister during the second stage of the bill were ominous. He noted that 'The purpose of regional authorities will be to promote the co-ordination of public, including local authority, services and the order establishing them will provide for a significant role in relation to the review and co-ordination of development plans.' The use of the verb 'promote' suggested a somewhat less directive role for the metropolitan council.

Granted, the 1993 legislation went further and Section 32 required the three new councils and Dublin Corporation to co-operate and to have due regard to the needs of the overall Dublin region in their policies and programmes. The managers of the Council areas were to ensure that necessary procedures would be in place to facilitate this. With this the minister was confident that the new structures would ensure that 'necessary co-ordination proceeds on an ongoing basis as regards local authority services and functions affecting the Dublin area as a whole'.

The new structures came into effect in 1994. As a consequence, 'County Dublin' ceased to exist, a fact probably unknown to most Dubliners. People still refer to 'County Dublin' and many activities are arranged on that spatial basis but it has no legal standing. The regional authority also came into existence but it cannot be said to have exercised much influence over the lives of the citizens of Dublin. In fact, it would be a safe bet that its existence was also unknown to most. Granted, it was now possible to discuss and debate issues that affected the city as a whole within a formal structure, but there was no means to enforce the implementation of the outcome of any such discussion. In yet another reform in 2014, it and the other regional authorities in Ireland were abolished and replaced by three regional assemblies. Dublin was now part of the Eastern and Midlands Regional Assembly, comprising the twelve local authorities in the area. Whatever the value of this, it cannot be said to provide the holistic overview a city the size of Dublin needs.

The oil refinery

It seems bizarre now that an oil refinery was ever contemplated for Dublin Bay yet people believed it was on the agenda in the late 1970s. Granted, by then the world had suffered two severe oil shocks that had sent prices soaring, making the vulnerability of the country to shortages very clear. Yet, the idea of building something as potentially dangerous as an oil refinery within the bounds of the capital city must be regarded as some kind of aberration. It is worth discussing here because it demonstrated how the governance structure of the city could produce odd results. The Port and Docks Board could have transformed a large portion of the city with little input from Dublin Corporation. Conversely, the bay could not be protected unless all of the councils agreed and acted in union.

The plan pre-dated the first oil crisis and first came to public attention in 1973 when the Dublin Bay Preservation Association broke the news that a refinery was being planned for a 200 acre (81ha) site in the South Wall/ Sandymount area of Dublin Bay. It claimed that the Port and Docks Board had been planning in secret for some time and that the minister was aware of it (*Evening Herald*, 20 March 1972, p. 3). They had been well briefed, even though the IDA denied that it had been in discussion about such a project (*Evening Herald*, 21 March 1972, p. 9). The answer to a question to the minister for local government in the Dáil on 22 March confirmed that 'commercial interests' had approached the Port and Docks Board about such a project but there was nothing definite yet. It was also confirmed that the necessary legislation would have to be complied with in terms of licensing and planning (*Irish Press*, 24 March, p. 9). There was no definite information during the spring and early summer but it was suggested that the project would cost £50m and would involve an Irish-French consortium. It was also rumoured that a berth of sorts would have to be built out at the Kish Bank in order to accommodate supertankers. The Dublin Bay Preservation Association took

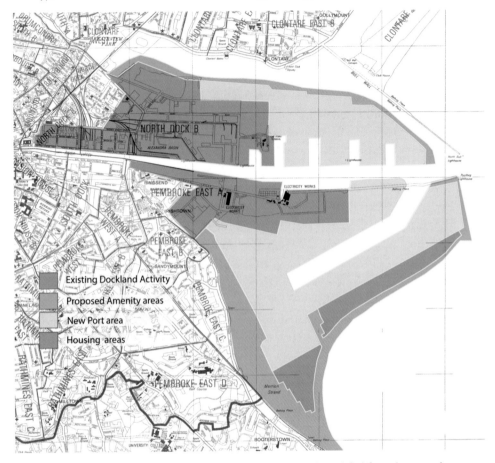

228 The proposed expansion of the port area. Redrawn and simplified from the original.

every opportunity to state its opposition and the residents' association in Sandymount saw both the proposed refinery and the proposed motorway (see next chapter) as significant threats. The proposals crystallized when the Port and Docks Board published their long awaited plan in July 1972. Except it was not called a 'plan', it was called 'studies' and presented as a series of options or possibilities for the future development of the port. Even though the idea of a refinery had raised concerns, the impact of what was being suggested took many people's breath away. The Board was suggesting filling in much of the bay and using it for industry and housing. On the southside, the bay would be filled in behind a line from Blackrock Baths to the Poolbeg lighthouse and on the northside from the Bull Wall to Fairview. The industrial elements would be built opposite Sandymount with multi-storey housing along the stretch to

Blackrock. On the northside, the land would be used for storage and transit. In all, the board would get 1,740 acres (704ha) on the south side (a Phoenix Park in essence) and 550 acres (222ha) on the north side. Screening would be provided by parks and trees but it was unclear who was going to provide these. It made the refinery plan seem modest in comparison. Reaction from the preservationist groups was swift and angry and if the Board thought there would be gentle consultations before the plan was implemented, they made a huge miscalculation. These 'studies' became a battleground for the next decade or more, with the refinery being only one of the more offensive elements.

To opposition from lobby groups was quickly added political opposition. The Labour Party's south-eastern Dublin constituency group was quick to reject the plan, saying that 'it was appalled at the values implicit in the published report' (*Irish Times*, 29 July 1972, p. 13). By early August, the Sandymount Fine Gael branch questioned the 'authority and moral right of the Port and Docks Board' to 'destroy for its own purposes' amenities such as Sandymount Strand (*Irish Times*, 4 August 1972, p. 13). The Confederation of Irish Industry was cautious in its response, saying that what was proposed did not fit with IDA plans (*Irish Times*, 17 August 1972, p. 6). One of the stated aims of the 'studies' was to generate interest and debate and in that they succeeded and the future of Dublin Bay became a live political and social topic. There were calls for a public inquiry into the plans and the issue even resulted in the formation of a cross-party parliamentary group comprised of TDs from the areas affected.

Into this febrile atmosphere came the long-awaited application for an oil refinery. It was announced in September that an application would be made for a refinery on a 200-acre site to be reclaimed by the Port and Docks Board, east of the ESB Generating Station. While the role of the Port and Docks Board was clear, there was an air of mystery about the project because the identity of those wishing to build the refinery would not be disclosed until permission was given, though it was suggested that Irish interests would be in the minority. The response was furious with Seán Loftus, legal representative to the Dublin Bay Preservation Association, rapidly becoming the public face of opposition. While that opposition might have been expected, a statement by the minister for transport and power, Brian Lenihan, that the government did not favour the proposal on grounds of regional planning, environmental and traffic concerns was not. The chairman of the Port and Docks Board professed himself 'shocked' at this news (*Irish Times*, 20 September 1972, p. 1). It was not all opposition. The Marine Port and General Workers' Union came

- its proposed location was such that it would involve an unacceptable risk of environmental damage and nuisance;
- the proposed development would be visually intrusive, obstruct views across the bay and detract from the open aspect of the bay and the amenity of Sandymount Strand;
- the public water supply was inadequate to satisfy the abnormally high requirement and accordingly the development was premature by reference to the existing deficiency in the provision of water supplies and the period within which such deficiency might reasonably be expected to be made good;
- the fire-protection facilities proposed were inadequate and the fire hazard involved was unacceptable because of the deficiencies in water supply, access and capacity to control a major oil fire or its spread to other properties.

The amenity order

One of the protections for Dublin Bay that was discussed during this period was the making of a special amenity order. This provided an extra layer of protection for locations with special and specific characteristics. Making an order was a complicated process. Firstly the Council had to pass a motion indicating that it wished to declare an area of special amenity. Dublin Corporation passed a motion supporting the making of an order but decided that the best way to ensure final approval was to commission a consultant's report on the bay. They got Brady, Shipman, Martin to map the area, indicating any boundary issues and suggesting developments that were compatible with the order. As mentioned above, Dún Laoghaire followed with a motion in 1974. This was still a long way from getting the protection in place. There needed to be agreement from Dublin County Council as well and, though there was no indication that it was opposed, it had yet to provide this.

That was only the first step. Having made an order, each council would have to hold a public inquiry since the order was bound to be opposed, and even then, the minister for local government had the final say. It took until 23 June 1975 before Dublin Corporation was in a position to make the order, with a strong expectation that it would be opposed. The general manager and secretary of the Dublin Port and Docks Board, J.P. Murphy, had written to Dublin Corporation members in the days prior to their meeting suggesting that there were dangers in making the order. The letter was quoted as saying: 'What I want to guard against is that industries which would provide employment and at the same time add to the amenities of Dublin would be turned away by all the obstructions sought to be imposed through the medium of an Amenity Order' (*Irish Times*, 21 June 1975, p. 13). It was February 1976 when Dublin County Council got to the point of making an order for that part of the bay under its jurisdiction.

None of the councils proceeded to hold public inquiries because, inter alia, they found themselves stymied by new legislation. Section 40 of the Local Government (Planning and Development) Act 1976 changed the definition of a special amenity area and the legal advice given to Dublin Corporation was that all three orders would have to be made again. So, despite all of the councils being in favour of an order, no order was in place while the refinery decision-making process was continuing. It was a prime example of the complexity of environmental protection in the 1970s, and also of the impact of the added layer of having three councils concerned. In the case of Dublin Corporation, the new order was made on 4 April 1977. As expected, there were objections and a public inquiry was held in 1978. This was subject to a temporary halt following a high court action to stop it completing its work. Paradoxically, Sean Loftus was now an objector, not because of any objection to the concept but because he felt that the order was not clear enough or useful enough. The fear was that though the particular refinery project had gone away there was nothing to stop it coming back. The process was eventually concluded but in 1981 the minister refused to confirm the order as 'being too vague' (SI No. 384/1981). All in all, it is a good job that it was not a crucial element in the defence against the refinery. By the end of the 1990s, only two such orders were in place – one for the Liffey Valley, made in 1987 and confirmed in 1990, and the second for the Bull Island, made in 1994 and approved in 1995.

The second oil crisis resulted in fears that the refinery idea would come back. For that reason, Mr Loftus sought on 8 February 1979, as a member of the Port and Docks Board, to get the Board to agree to a resolution that would have prevented it from supporting a future refinery project. This was defeated on the grounds that it would pre-empt future Board decisions, which was exactly what Mr Lofus was trying to do. So, the refinery idea slipped into abeyance but never quite went away. It was replaced briefly, though, by another bizarre idea. This was the creation of an underground storage cavern in Dublin Port for Liquid Petroleum Gas. This was given permission by Dublin Corporation, but objections resulted in a public planning appeal which began on 22 February 1983. This proposal ultimately went away too, but from today's perspective it is hard to fathom why anyone would contemplate such potentially explosive storage in the heart of a city.

A tale of the car and the bus

There are many perennial issues in the story of Dublin and coping with traffic has been one such since almost the beginning. Dublin developed a radial circulation system that focused on a small number of crossing points on the river. As the city grew to the east, the bridging was not adjusted to suit the emerging city and the work of the Wide Streets Commissioners, while marvellous in many ways, did not help. The main axis of the modern city centre, which they developed, runs parallel to the river along Dame Street and only crosses the river at what became O'Connell Bridge. Flows were concentrated into the relatively narrow junction where College Green meets Westmoreland Street. From the beginning this was a pinch point. The city moved east but so did the port, for reasons of its own. It was not a synchronized process and there was resistance to providing bridging points east of O'Connell Bridge because of the loss of berthage. A further complication was that the port developed on both sides of the river, though with a concentration on the north side. Intra-port traffic resulted in flows up and down the quays where it mingled with city-centre traffic. Managing these flows and solving the increasing congestion became an important pre-occupation for the city authorities in the nineteenth century and into the twentieth. Efforts were not particularly successful and city-centre congestion only got worse as more and more private cars began to appear in the urban landscape.

Then there was the wider question of planning the road network for the city. The radial nature of the road system was naturally focused on the city centre, so the emphasis was on trying to develop a system that modified the radials by developing circular roads. The aim was to keep people on less crowded routes for as long as possible until they really needed to plunge into the city centre. Various combinations of radials and circular routes featured in the plans of Abercrombie and others during the first half of the twentieth century. Some were built but there was not a coherent or consistent approach to road building.

If the first five decades of the twentieth century were characterized by slow progress (if any) in the development of the transportation network, then the next two decades were positively frenzied, at least in terms of the plans. The era of the traffic-planning consultant began with the Schaechterle plan for the city at the beginning of the 1960s, followed quickly by Myles Wright.

229 A busy O'Connell Street at the end of the 1960s.

The Dublin Transportation Study, the subject of this chapter, followed in the early years of the 1970s. This involved a more holistic view of 'transportation' than roads but it prompted Dublin Corporation to commission the R. Travers Morgan Company to develop detailed proposals for the road network within its area. These were discussed in volume 7, *Dublin in the 1950s and 1960s: cars, shops and suburbs* (pp 209–17) and will be mentioned only in passing here.

Each of these plans envisaged road building on a massive scale, with motorways reaching right into the city centre and multi-level roads becoming a feature of the central area, as was the case in many European cities. The canals came under threat. They were ready-made routeways and the era of canal traffic was over. It made sense, it seemed, to give the routes new purposes as six lane (or more) highways. Demolition in the centre was not seen as a particular problem either. There was a great deal of decay and dereliction, which seemed to indicate that Dubliners were not really bothered about their urban fabric.

None of the more dramatic elements of these plans was ever built; the money did not exist. Moreover, it seemed also that a plan was no sooner complete and presented than it was found necessary to revise the assumptions under which it was made and make a new plan.

The plan for the 1970s was the 'Dublin Transportation Study'. This grew out of a parallel process to the planning of Dublin Corporation. As early as 1966, the department of local government had identified a need for traffic surveys as part as the process of producing development plans and set about identifying the towns in which these should take place. Dún Laoghaire and Bray were recognized as needing such studies, especially as Schaechterle's remit had not extended as far south. It was realized that it made no sense to study these in isolation since they were part of a network that included south Dublin and there were two major arterial roads in the area – the Bray Road and the Merrion Road/Rock Road. This suggested to the planners that there should be a study that would embrace the south-east of Dublin and the north of Wicklow, an area bounded by the Enniskerry Road to the sea and from the Dodder to Greystones.

Of course, if it made no sense to isolate these towns from south-east Dublin, it made equally no sense to isolate this area from the rest of the city. They came up with a convoluted rationale that the Myles Wright proposals were still under consideration and that these dealt with the entire region, while Dublin Corporation, County Dublin and Dún Laoghaire were all producing development plans for what could be seen as being sub-regions. This being so, it was more unclear why Dún Laoghaire merited special attention. The real reason for concentrating on the sub-region chosen was that of cost. The Schaechterle study had been dismissed as dealing only with traffic, nevermind the furore his proposals generated. Increasingly, it was suggested that a distinction was drawn between 'traffic' and 'transportation', though this was not often explained well since the terms were used interchangeably. However, when the distinction was drawn, 'traffic' could be seen as the outcome of 'transportation policy'. So the thinking, at the time, was that urban transportation planning had to investigate the relationship between land use and travel. In other words, they had to look at the geography of the city and see where people needed to travel and suggest policies affecting both places and flows. It was not just a matter of deciding how best to link locations; land use planning and zoning could have a profound effect on the management of flows of traffic. Part of this process involved doing extensive surveys of peoples' travel patterns. This was particularly expensive and an unwillingness to spend this kind of money is what drove the decision to do a sub-regional study.

At that time, An Foras Forbartha was receiving assistance from the United Nations Special Fund and it was decided to capitalize on this by asking An Foras Forbartha to take on the study. So, early in 1967 they sought UN aid and this resulted in a scoping study that did not challenge the area to be studied but rather looked at structures that might be used to undertake the study. Part of that was the recruitment of an international consultant who would be the team leader, the study director. This proved to be a difficulty and it took until 1970 before a study director arrived in Dublin. By this point, the conclusion had been reached that the Myles Wright report was not going to be implemented in full and an early decision was that this new study should have its remit extended to encompass all of Dublin, common sense winning out at last and for once! Thus was born the 'Dublin Transportation Study'.

A multi-agency team was assembled from the three councils, CIÉ and An Foras Forbartha and detailed work began in 1970 with a final report completed in November 1971. This contained recommendations on roads, public transportation, development, parking, plan implementation and updating. It was notable that this report was produced by people working in the region and not outside consultants. It meant that local knowledge could be used effectively. As well as a report that set out the recommendations, there was a volume of twenty-two technical reports that described the methodology and the decision-making process.

The analysis was comprehensive, with much stress testing of the various scenarios. It suffered, of course, like all predictive exercises, in that judgment (or guessing) was necessary about what would happen to car ownership and other economic indicators in the period to 1991 – the date for which the system was being generated. They were also conscious of an increasingly sceptical public and a degree of militancy among middle-class residents. They had seen and understood what had happened to the proposals for the Grand Canal and Georgian Dublin and shied away from anything dramatic there.

The preferred outcome was for a circumferential motorway system, enclosing the city. This would run from the south of the airport around the city in the space between the built up area and the new towns. It would swing east at Rathcoole and continue around the edge of the city until it headed south towards Bray and Wicklow at Sandyford. The aim was to divert traffic from the city that did not need to be there and this would link the main north–south and east–west routes. This generated relatively little comment

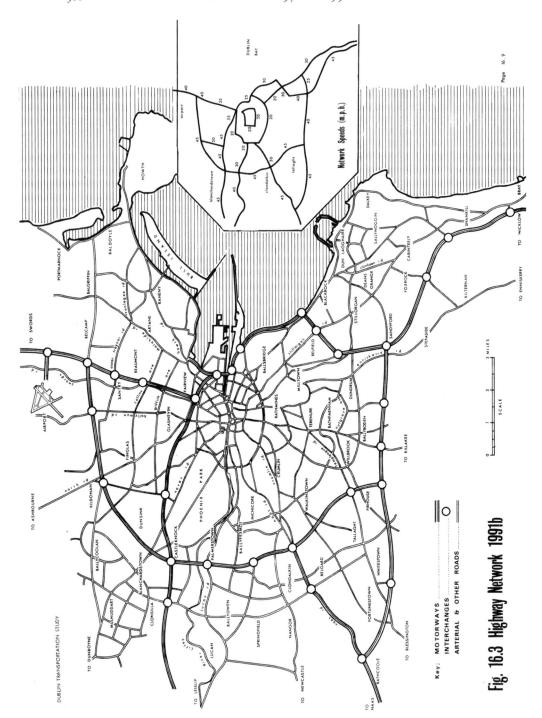

230 DTS: the preferred road system. (DTS, 1972, fig. 16.3.)

or opposition because the land was undeveloped. Much more controversial was the eastern side where the land was built up. As with the other plans, within the motorway system would be two inner rings, which would further distribute traffic, bringing it closer to its destination before taking it into the centre. The outer ring followed roughly the circular roads while the inner ring was not greatly dissimilar to the tangent ring envisaged by the Schaechterle study.

The issue was how to get the traffic from the outer ring to the inner rings. There were certainly plenty of radials already but it was felt that none had the capacity that was needed. So the decision was to create a small number of motorway routes into the central area.

The Grand Canal itself was relatively safe. The Draft Development plan recognized its amenity value and there was certainly no political will to draw the ire of the local residents again. However, it was suggested that it would be possible to upgrade the adjacent road system and make use of the direct route that the canal provided. Technical Report 20 discussed the various options. One was a one-way system on the existing network. Another was a variant on this with a two- or three-lane one-way system on either side of the canal, increased by one lane at the major intersections. The final option was a four-lane route on the south side of the canal with grade separation at the intersections with the main radial routes. Not surprisingly the more extensive road systems would accommodate more cars and capacity would range from 14,500 passenger car units using the existing roads to over 40,000 for a grade-separated four-lane road. Of course, these would require more demolition and be much more intrusive on the landscape, though the canal itself would lose very little under any of the proposals. The recommended solution understood the realities quite well. There would be a 24-foot carriageway on each side of the canal from Mount Street Bridge to Griffith Bridge (at the junction of the current R111, the end of the circular section of the canal). Traffic going east would use the northern side of the canal. This would not be without loss on the northern side of the canal and would have required the demolition of ten cottages on Portobello Road as well as the loss of much garden space. However, there was no need to extend these roads further west as the existing network was deemed suitable.

It was a different story with the Royal Canal. It was unloved and newspaper reports during the early 1970s referred to it in unflattering terms, as an 'open sewer', a 'rat-infested dump' and 'an eyesore'. There were regular calls to fill it in, to clean it up, for CIÉ to get rid of it. Typical of the coverage was the *Irish Independent*, 13 September 1972 (p. 10). Running a motorway along the canal route generated mostly positive reactions initially. The plan did not specifically mention filling it in; the reference was to the 'canal route', but anyone who knew the canal also knew that a motorway would occupy the entire cutting and more. This motorway also had very few interchanges and the one at 'Castleknock' and 'Navan Road' (Cabra) could be accommodated without much disruption. This was not the case with the proposed interchange at Drumcondra, where the motorway would meet the extension of the northern arm of the network (the current M1). While much of the route would be through undeveloped land, this would change once the system got to Drumcondra. The canal motorway would be six lanes here and it would meet the 'airport' arm at Jones' Road. As Technical Report 16 put it 'the section of the motorway between the interchange with Dorset Street and the New Liffey Bridge poses problems from the geometric design point of view. This is because there are two interchanges within 0.4 miles and the turning and weaving movements are large' (p. 16.15). This too seemed to be initially acceptable.

In addition to these major roads, there would be a system of collector and distributor roads. These would have two main functions. Firstly they would send traffic onto the motorways and so take it out of residential areas. They would also link residential areas, shopping centres and new industrial sites.

However, it was the eastern arm of the circular system that generated the most attention almost immediately. The motorway system would feed traffic in towards the city centre, which would be bypassed via a Liffey bridge, before being fed southwards along a coastal motorway, which would swing south-westwards at the edge of Belfield before completing the circle at Sandyford and sending traffic on the way towards Wicklow. The new Liffey bridge had been in contemplation for a long time. It was now almost a century since a bridge had been built to the east of O'Connell Street. Everyone agreed that such a bridge was badly needed but it had not proved possible to put all of the necessary elements together – the agreement of the three councils, the Dublin Port and Docks Board, and the necessary finance. It had appeared in the sketch development plan published in 1941 and a detailed proposal was part of the Myles Wright plan (see Brady, 2014). It was another element that was always going to be in the DTS. So much so, that Dublin Corporation had undertaken a parallel process, keeping the DTS in the loop, seeking a design for such a bridge while the Dublin Transportation Study was underway and it received its report in December 1972, a month after the DTS report. The

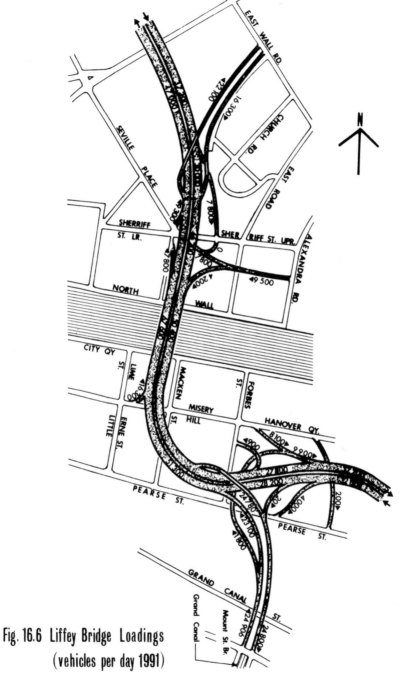

Fig. 16.6 Liffey Bridge Loadings
(vehicles per day 1991)

231 The road system at the new Liffey bridge. The figure shows the loadings expected in 1991.
(DTS, 1972, fig. 16.6.)

plan was for a low-level bridge that would cross the Liffey between Spencer Dock and Grand Canal Dock, around Macken Street. Even in the early 1970s, these were increasingly marginal to CIÉ's operations and it would be possible to accommodate the necessary interchanges without too much disruption, though some housing would have to go. An additional element would be a high-capacity link between Clontarf Road and Spencer Dock. This would run behind Fairview Park and was designed to divert non-city bound traffic away from the North Strand route in the city. There would be a significant loss of berthage, the days of transporter or lift bridges was gone, but increasingly the business of the port was being done to the east of the likely location.

The issue now was what to do with the traffic once it crossed from north to south. Sensitivities about the Georgian landscape had increased to the point that there was now no question of running a motorway through that part of the city; it would just have to cope with the inner tangents. So, that just left the coastal route. It was also inconceivable to attempt to run a motorway through the heart of the emerging business centre and leafy Ballsbridge. Having a road along the strand at Sandymount would take care of these problems. By definition, it was undeveloped land and anyway there were all sorts of suggestions in the air about filling it in and using it for industrial development. In fact, these suggestions had been around since the 1930s when it was proposed that the airport for Dublin should be sited there. A proposal was emerging for an oil refinery combined with a large high-rise residential element. Looking back, with the benefit of hindsight, it seems remarkable that any agency felt that they would get away with this. Residents' associations had been mobilized and energized by the Grand Canal campaign and the developing Wood Quay campaign. The residents of Sandymount were particularly aware of the threats to the neighbourhood and they were also well resourced both in terms of money and political influence.

The inner tangent ring was designed to make traffic flows work in the very heart of the city. Such a ring had been described by Schaechterle, and the DTS proposals differed in detail but not in kind. The route would take traffic along Parnell Street, North King Street and into Smithfield where it would head towards the Liffey and across it via Queen Maeve Bridge (later Mellows Bridge). On the other side of the Liffey it would make use of Bridgefoot Street and onwards until it reached the Coombe whence it would head east linking up with the southern routes along New Street/Clanbrassil Street and Camden Street. This route had the advantage of passing through much derelict and unused land. It was also outside the action spaces of most Dubliners, with the exception of Parnell Street, and therefore did not impinge greatly on their sense of the city. The most controversial element of any form of the inner tangent would be the eastern leg which would link the St Stephen's Green area with the Parnell/O'Connell Street area. This would pass near or through the Georgian core of the city. Once again, combining pragmatism with analysis, the study was able to determine that the proposed system could function without any fundamental change to the urban landscape (p. 8.7). Dublin Corporation gave the job of fleshing out the detail of this system to R. Travers Morgan and it was really only then that the full impact of these plans began to be understood by the public.

Public transport

After decades of indecision, the study affirmed that enhanced public transport was a necessary element in the development of the city. A key element of land-use planning was that employment should be located only where there was good public transport. This could be done by allowing moderately higher plot ratios (the ratio of floor area to surface area) for major office and commercial developments located within the inner tangent ring and the Georgian area to the east. At the same time it was recognized that 'it would not be possible to permit all the cars that are available for use to enter the city centre at all times' (p. 18.1). There was no doubt that the motorway system would be more dramatic in visual impact. After all, some 70 miles of motorway and 105 miles of arterial roads were planned. Public transport, though, needed to improve both in terms of the system and the level of service. This would involve buses but also re-animation of the almost defunct railway system.

There needed to be a system of high-speed bus routes that would operate within the new towns and on three radial routes to the city centre. The routes would comprise a mixture of busways, bus lanes and reserved streets that could be used only by buses during peak hours. The Harcourt Street line would become a busway from Leopardstown to the city centre with interchanges at intervals where buses could join the route and passengers could switch routes. The northern route would use the airport motorway with connections to the west and east to serve Ballymun and Darndale. Some of the access points would be for buses only.

The DTS also advocated bus lanes at peak times. The report accepted that the recent experiments at Fairview had not generated unanimous enthusiasm. The authors felt that work could be done on making these lanes more flexible so that more traffic could be accommodated and that the basis for judgment of the value of any proposal should be on the number of people carried and not the number of vehicles.

The plan envisaged that the major share of city-centre-bound traffic would be by public transport, while that in the suburbs would be largely by private vehicles. This would capitalize on the system that was already in place, which was largely radial and focused on the city centre. However, they recognized that there were issues with the current bus system. As they put it:

> While recognizing the dominance of peak hour capacity and congestion problems, continuing emphasis should be placed on improving the efficiency of all bus operations. Such improvements would aim at better running to schedule and closer monitoring of overload points, thus minimizing the bypassing of passengers. Radio control of buses at present being examined seems an essential first step to improve the bus operations. Buses are the principal means of transport other than cycles or walking for the 50% of the families in the area who do not own cars and/or the 25% who will not own them in 1991. Also of concern are the old and infirm and others who cannot drive and are wholly dependent on public transport.
>
> (*Transportation in Dublin*, 1971)

The later consultative committee would make much the same point but would put it in more direct terms. The report also addressed the lack of a central bus station. It did not settle on a particular location, though it knew that CIÉ was looking at both sides of the quays around the Ha'penny Bridge, but it did accept the need for such a facility and that it needed preferential access by means of reserved streets at peak times.

The study suggested that the two existing rail corridors through Blanchardstown and Clondalkin be upgraded for suburban services and that the existing suburban services should be upgraded to provide better peak-time capacity and that they should run all day.

These seem modest proposals and it is an indication of just how far public transport had fallen from the transport agenda. There was little enthusiasm for the idea of providing Dublin with an underground. It would simply divert people from other public transport, and while the study could not say whether it might be needed after 1991, there was certainly no need for it until then. It did concede that there might be virtue in a short underground in central

Dublin to link the existing rail terminals and it suggested an immediate investigation into this. One of the outcomes was that such a line appeared on the maps of the Dublin Development Plan.

Parking

The car had to be managed in the city centre and this required detailed planning of parking provision. Control measures were already in place and Dubliners were getting used to parking meters in the best parking locations. The DTS study of parking demand was comprehensive and reported in Technical Report 11. It predicted that the demand for parking spaces in an unconstrained central business district in 1991 would be 145,000, comprising 32,000 long-term and 113,000 short-term or non-work-related spaces. Their comparable analysis for 1971 suggested that the demand was for just under 59,000. The DTS view was very simple: 'the existing facilities could not cope with this [projected] demand' (pp 11–19). However, it was more muted in what to do about that. The report agreed that what was needed was (a) an increase in turnover in parking spaces and (b) a restraint on demand. The latter would be achieved by shifting the split between public and private transport, whereas all they had to say about turnover was that control measures (parking meters) should be extended to cover all on-street parking. On-street parking should be removed in the most congested areas as off-street parking became available. It was a far-cry from the coercive and anti-car measures which are much more favoured today. These proposals would get close to demand as long as the multi-storey car parks, which were adopted later in the development plan, were built. This envisaged 1,250 spaces at Waterford Street, 1,000 at Moore Street, 800 at York Street and 300 at Nassau Street. Demand could be met by producing long-term parking at the edge of the city centre, within walking distance. It was a balance that would not now find much support.

The new towns

Recognizing the important role of public transport was a step change from the inconsistent approaches of the 1960s when it was unclear what role it would or could play in a society with increasing access to cars. However, the DTS largely confined itself to high-level statements rather than detailed specific proposals, largely because it would fall to CIÉ to devise and implement the necessary changes. Technical Report 21, though, was an analysis of the possibilities for public transport in Tallaght and it provides an indication of the thinking at the time. This study was not part of the DTS; rather, it was another independent strand, which, to their credit, the project team wove into the whole. The study was completed by Dublin City Bus services before the DTS. It used a different methodology and its baselines were somewhat different, but the DTS was happy to (a) report on its findings and (b) comment that its figures 'are remarkably close to those quoted elsewhere for the Tallaght area in other Technical Reports'.

The Myles Wright proposals for Tallaght and the other new towns envisaged high-density, highly planned communities. He believed that people would insist on using their cars but there would be ample opportunities for people to both walk and to use public transport. The plans that were emerging for Tallaght did not follow this high-density model but the technical report suggested that the large volume of traffic generated within Tallaght and between Tallaght and the other settlements could be accommodated by public transport, though only with a high standard of service. The road system would not be capable of accommodating this since the neighbourhood system being used, with its controlled access, would require a large number of circuitous low-frequency routes. Instead something new and targeted would be necessary.

Various examples of high-tech approaches were considered such as the Cabtrack System – automatically controlled small vehicles moving on segregated guideways – or the Dashaveyor system, ultimately deployed at the Toronto Zoo. These were cutting-edge applications but they remained unproven at the time in a large-scale urban setting. They were rejected, in any event, because they were too expensive to be contemplated.

Instead, this study looked, as Wright had undoubtedly done, to the British new town programme and especially the system of busways being developed in Runcorn. The proposal for Tallaght was that it would get a busway (a dedicated road for buses) to meet local needs, which would link with a busway to the city. The advantage of the busway was that it could integrate into the road system when that made sense and that it could also deliver people directly into shopping districts and perhaps even have first-floor access points.

The system envisaged for Tallaght was a figure-of-eight system, as in Runcorn, and this would serve all the residential districts to the west of the town centre and incorporate the Whitestown Industrial Estate. It would be almost entirely busway. The eastern component would use existing roads to serve the areas north of the Dodder. Because of the terrain south of the Dodder, it would be necessary to connect with the town centre by a distinct and separate route. In addition, there would be two short peak-time links to the industrial estates at Cookstown and Airton. It made most sense to have a

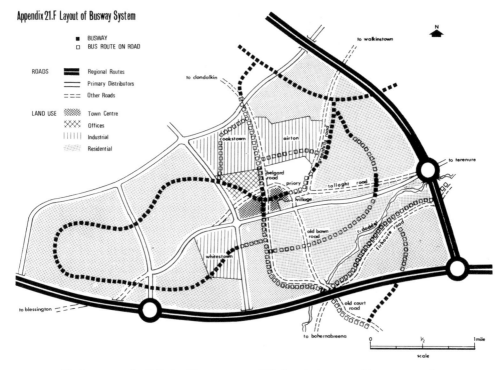

232 The bus system for Tallaght. The system would link with the external bus routes in the centre. (DTS, 1972, 21.F.)

dual system, with local services bringing people to a central hub from which they could travel to other centres or to the city.

There was nothing earth-shattering in this proposal, as it had been promoted in the Myles Wright report. It would require considerable capital expenditure as it involved 16 miles (26km) of routes, 9 miles (14.5km) of which was a separate busway, but this would be nothing compared to that required for the more hi-tech approaches. The report sounded a warning, which could have been applied more generally and not just to transport. It was noted that:

> the fragmented nature of the development which is taking place at the moment in Tallaght will make the operation of public transport very difficult in the next few years. Housing development is taking place now in at least four areas, which are not served adequately by any existing route. The scattered locations of these areas will make them very dependent on public transport when they are completed. Yet the number of houses is not great enough in any of the areas to warrant

a good service and their locations will necessitate each being served by a separate route. It would be most desirable in the development of the other satellite towns that building should take place in an orderly manner so that the housing estates when completed could be served by progressive extensions of the bus route or routes.

(p. 21.6)

Phasing

This was a twenty-year plan and nobody expected that the money would be available quickly. At the same time, it was recognized that phasing was important to ensure that projects were integrated. The DTS view was that 'the most immediate problems are in the city centre and the approaches thereto'. To that end, 'the most single relief that can be obtained is the building of the eastern bypass of the city centre' (p. 18.5). To that was added the need to get public transport up to required levels by upgrading the rail system and by providing the busways from Leopardstown, Finglas, Ballymun and Darndale because 'it is necessary to provide people with an acceptable and attractive alternative to the car for commuting purposes' (p. 18.6).

The proposed sequencing involved four phases. In the first phase, the eastern bypass would be completed, together with the airport link from Whitehall. There would also be work done on the roads from Bray into Dublin and on the Belfast Road. Phase 1 would end in 1979 and the next phase of only three years would involve the building of the western leg of the motorway ring from Tallaght to Castleknock. This was 'absolutely' necessary to integrate the three new towns and to ensure their linkages while breaking any linkage with the centre. At the end of 1983 there would be 'a basic north-south bypass of the city on the east and west, which together will contribute towards re-orienting traffic patterns from the (undesirable) radial pattern which causes arterial congestion to a (more desirable) circumferential pattern' (p. 18.6).

The third phase would last until 1986 and this would continue the integration of the circular system with the connection along the Royal Canal linking up with the motorway from Whitehall. In phase 4, the southern leg of the motorway would be completed from Ballycullen to Sandyford and from Ballycullen to Tallaght. The northern motorway would link up with the western leg by an extension from the airport to Blake's Cross and to this would be added a portion of the south-eastern leg from Loughlinstown to Valery Bridge, south of Bray.

As this point in 1991, the basic network would be complete and work could focus on the completion of the system. The various arterials and linkages would be constructed in tandem with the motorways. Additionally, while the recommendations did not include the extension of the southern coast route beyond Booterstown, it would be prudent to provide for extension to Blackrock and onwards to Dún Laoghaire by protecting the route from development. In similar mode, though the motorway from Irishtown to Booterstown was recommended as a two-lane dual motorway, it would be sensible to plan for its expansion to six lanes in total if the extension to Blackrock became necessary.

The DTS recognized that the fragmentation of responsibility posed a significant challenge. They identified five road authorities, one semi-state body and three government departments that had responsibilities for transportation in the Dublin region. They recommended a co-ordinating committee but later proposals would go much further.

Reaction

As already discussed in the chapter on governance, it was the eastern bypass, the single most crucial element according to the DTS, that generated the most controversy. Opposition to it was instantaneous and given greater impetus by the parallel oil refinery proposal. Dublin Corporation, after much debate, inserted a line into its development plan indicating that it would follow the recommendations of the Dublin Transportation Study but the fate of the eastern bypass was sealed by then. Dún Laoghaire Corporation voted to exclude their segment of the road from their development plan on 5 February 1979. This would stop the road, dead in its tracks, at Booterstown with no route to the southern leg of the circular motorway. The reasons stated were a lack of consultation by Dublin Corporation on the plan and a concern for the bird sanctuary at Booterstown. The former could be smoothed but nothing could be done about the latter, though a complete redesign of the roadway might have been possible. This was a very public manifestation of the problems caused by the fractured governance of the city, but on this occasion it was welcomed by many. As discussed in the previous chapter, Dublin Corporation persisted with plans for the road for a while but it was ultimately abandoned at its meeting on 26 May 1980. This meeting also decided not to proceed with a number of the inner-city tangent routes, including Summerhill, Parnell Street, North King Street, Bridgefoot Street, Cork Street, Ardee Street, Cuffe Street and Kevin Street. While there was a clear majority of 23 to 15 for the vote on the eastern bypass, the vote on the tangent routes was split and required the casting vote of the lord mayor, William Cumiskey. In fact, it was too late

233 The wide road at Bridgefoot Street going nowhere in 1994.

to do anything along much of the inner tangent routes. The land had been reserved and was derelict in many cases and building had commenced. What resulted was a more or less connected set of tangent elements but with some lonely and isolated stretches, such as at Bridgefoot Street. As it rises from the Liffey quays with two lanes, it becomes a dual carriageway after its junction with Usher Street but loses that capacity after its junction with Thomas Street. The impressive width of North King Street disappears once it crosses Church Street. On the southside, however, the impact of the tangent route is evident from the South Circular Road all the way to Christ Church.

The canals were saved. The planning committee voted on 6 March 1980 that no major roads would run on either canal. The Council could have reversed the canal vote but it chose not to. As a result, there was no road building on the Royal Canal and therefore nothing to connect with the motorway spur from Whitehall, and it too fell by the wayside. What was intended as a motorway ultimately became the Port Tunnel, designed now to divert port-bound traffic from the city's streets. At the same meeting, it was decided to

236 The chassis building works at Inchicore in the 1950s.

to five minutes at peak times. Electrification was seen as not only modern but also important in reducing dependence on oil at a time when Ireland's vulnerability was once more being demonstrated. The electric system would also be quieter, it was argued, and would have less impact on the environment.

Work commenced quickly, though not quite immediately, and it was reported in April 1980 that track laying was underway on the first section between Killester and Howth Junction (*Irish Times*, 3 April 1980, p. 1). There was an expectation at that time that the carriages would be built in Inchicore under the direction of the German company Linke Hoffman Busch. CIÉ had a long tradition of coach building in Inchicore and its chassis production facility designed by Michael Scott and built by G. & T. Crampton in the late 1940s was regarded as a masterpiece of industrial design. This did not happen and the train sets were built in Germany and shipped complete to Dublin.

By November 1982, it was reported that 80 per cent of the track works were complete (*Irish Times*, 5 November 1982, p. 15). Given the age of railway in central Dublin it was not surprising that eleven junctions with the road system were at grade, with a system of manually operated gates. This would no longer serve and it was necessary to install an automatic system, which would be centrally controlled and monitored. The frequency of the new system would necessitate that the barriers would be closed very often, with consequent disruption to traffic, especially at peak times. This was all the more so because CIÉ decided to give a longer 'lead-in' time to train arrival than would be common in large cities in Europe, perhaps because they understood Dubliners a bit better. Most of the junctions were in residential areas because of the line followed by the railway. There was one junction, though, where it was predicted to be a problem and so it turned out to be. The coastal road from Irishtown joined with the Ballsbridge to Blackrock Road at Merrion Gates; the name said it all. It was suggested that a grade-separated junction was needed here but this was rejected on cost grounds. Traffic patterns adapted to the changed circumstances, but it remains one of the traffic pinch-points in the suburbs.

Almost immediately, pressure came to extend the line to Greystones. It was argued that the contractors were on site and it would be far more efficient to have them do the work now than to have to come back to it later. Money was short, shorter than usual, and there was resistance from the various government departments, even though the project was grant-aided by the European Regional Development Fund. Perhaps some of the resistance arose from the realization that Bray–Greystones was only one of the extensions being lobbied for. CIÉ itself proposed a major extension in 1983 when it unveiled proposals (reanimating some of the earlier proposals discussed above) to electrify a line from Tallaght through Kilnamanagh to the Naas Road and then towards the city via Cherry Orchard, Ballyfermot and Inchicore to a new station at St John's Road, Heuston Station. This would easily integrate into their plans for the underground and thus with the new Dublin public transport system (*Irish Times*, 30 April 1983, p. 1).

As the line was nearing completion, plans were announced for the feeder bus system. Single-decker buses, in the system livery, would run from Blackrock and Dún Laoghaire on the south side, and Raheny, Sutton and Harmonstown on the north side. This was important because the DART was a coastal line for most of its route and it was believed that people would not accept much inconvenience in using it. Having these feeders was estimated to increase the catchment area for the system to 200,000. There would also be a circular route linking the central stations – Connolly, Pearse, Heuston and Tara Street – until the underground was built!

Everything was set fair for a gentle launch in April 1983. Dubliners learned in February that they would be travelling on the DART – Dublin Area Rapid Transit. Unusually, this was an English-language acronym, but it was catchy and indicated speed and direction. They were also introduced to an American concept – park and ride – whereby they would be encouraged to drive to a car park adjacent to a station and transfer to the DART, thereby reducing the flows on the roads. Alas, the launch was delayed by one of the elements the Consultative Commission had referred to – industrial relations. The introduction was seen by the various unions as a golden opportunity to improve the working conditions of drivers and it took until July before a satisfactory settlement was found. This allowed the DART system to begin on 23 July, though a separate industrial-relations process ensured that the feeder buses did not appear at the same time.

Dubliners took to the DART immediately and it was reported at the end of August that 40,000 passengers were already using it every day, a considerable increase on the 30,000 or so who used the old system and it was confidently expected that the system would grow to serve 80,000 per day. What was unclear, however, was how many of these passengers would be new public-transport users and how many would be just people deflected from the buses. Indeed, CIÉ expected that there would be reduced bus usage along the DART line and made plans to reduce capacity. There seems to have been a missed opportunity to 'encourage' more car users to take advantage of the new system by introducing more control measures in the city centre.

The system at the end of the 1980s

The major change in the period discussed here was the decline in the belief that urban motorways were necessary or useful. At the beginning of the period, it was argued that it was necessary to have high-capacity roads bringing traffic into the city centre. By the end of the 1980s, it was accepted that this was no longer desirable. The change in emphasis can be seen in the various reports discussed above as the cost and the environmental impact pushed the projects out of the realm of what was possible. Residents were no longer prepared to contemplate the impact on their neighbourhoods of massive constructions and they proved very effective in preventing them. Additionally, it was understood that no amount of road building would ever meet the insatiable demands of the car. Dublin still had a long way to go to match car ownership in other prosperous cities and that realization was a potent factor in tempering plans.

237 The M50 facilitated the edge city.

238 Clanbrassil Street looking south before widening.

Public transport came to be seen as being much more important. Having been downplayed and mostly ignored during the 1960s, it came to be understood that an efficient public-transport system was needed to make the city function properly. It was also recognized that what Dublin had was far from efficient and making it efficient was a major concern of the reports discussed here.

Dublin did not get its urban motorways but the peripheral routes were seen as important and it eventually got its peripheral motorway, what is now called the M50. This was to have a profound effect on the land-use patterns of the city and allowed, as it was intended to do, an 'edge city' to emerge, where large-scale industry and retail was located on the edge. This resulted in the city being turned inside-out in large measure, with flows directed outwards from the older city to these new edge developments. It was also too late to prevent many elements of the inner-city tangent road projects becoming a reality. These went ahead in many cases, producing wide boulevards such as along Clanbrassil Street and Patrick Street.

In some respects it was the worst of all worlds. Elements of wide streets were produced but they did not join up so traffic eventually found itself moving in and out of chicanes. The best (or worst) example has to be North King Street, where the road widens after Bolton Street to four lanes plus two cycle tracks, only to be faced with two lanes and no cycle tracks across the junction with Church Street. The solution found here was a complex and confusing system of one-way streets. Elsewhere, elements of the road systems were built. Three commuter bridges had been built to the east of Butt Bridge, ending a century of contemplation. The Talbot Memorial Bridge was opened in 1978 followed by the east link (Tom Clarke) bridge in 1984. The latter was provided with a wide approach road on the north side but the opposite on the south side. The Samuel Beckett Bridge, which opened in 2009, completed the set of crossings that had been the subject of such debate. The airport motorway morphed into the port tunnel some years later, but the Royal Canal now serves an amenity purpose. While control measures increased in the city centre and bus lanes became commonplace, the busways did not appear, nor did the underground. The routes discussed for busways, though, formed the kernel of the light-rail Luas system which arrived in 2004.

There were other initiatives designed to improve the attractiveness and efficiency of public transport. 'Quality Bus Corridors', a version of the busway but not as segregated, became a reality in the 1990s. Cityswift buses appeared on the landscape. These were high-capacity (70-passenger) single-decker buses designed to run on Quality Bus Corridors (QBCs), properly demarcated

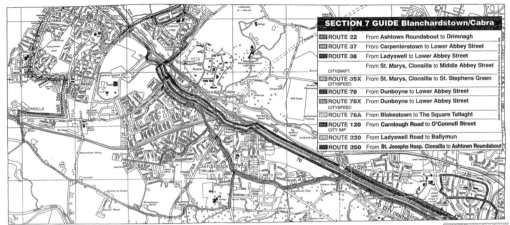

Pioneer on the Quality Corridor

THE NEW Cityswift service from Blanchardstown is pioneering the Dublin Bus Quality Corridor concept — and is a prototype for at least another nine corridors in the city.

The No 39 bus is the first to wear the Cityswift logo and the first to take the new single deck bus into service.

The new buses, which carry 71 passengers, are lavishly equipped with a new "green" diesel engine, soft styled interiors and on board infra red devices to signal traffic lights should to stay green — or change from red to go.

Over the past few months, bus drivers on the new Cityswift route have undergone a two day course in customer relations — an aspect Dublin Bus is keen to improve.

The new bus will run every six minutes from 7 am — 7 pm. The new Cityswift will operate the route currently taken by route 39X and will therefore bypass Castleknock. But the people of Castleknock are not forgotten. The frequency on route 37 will be increased to Laurel Lodge and Carpenterstown.

With a new terminus at Clonsilla, the 39s will now continue onto the old Navan Road as far as Auburn Ave, then to the dual carriageway and into the city — a more direct route than before, Dublin Bus says.

A special school service will aim to keep schoolchildren off the Cityswift in peak hours: children generally make short journeys and pay a fraction of the adult fare.

Children currently being carried on route 39 will be facilitated on the schools network, thereby leaving seats available for people going to work. A special school service will also operate in conjunction with route 38.

But, in a change to its route, the bus will now travel from Berkeley Road into Blessington St., Parnell Sq. and terminate in the city centre — a much more direct journey.

The route 70 serving Clones and Dunboyne will have a significantly improved frequency.

Currently, in the Cabra area, the 22 and 22A is a cross city double deck route. Now the 22 will not actually go into Cabra, but bypass it along the new Cabra Road and go onto the Navan Road, where it will terminate.

Cabra itself will be served by a new high frequency City Imp service — along the lines of the successful No 83, the first City Imp. The Cabra City Imp, route 120, will run to the city centre every 7-10 minutes.

There will be five No 39x Cityspeed services in the morning peak, an expressway-type bus which runs 07.15am — 8 00am.It will also have its frequency increased by one extra bus morning and evening.

Dublin Bus says that because of the changes, there will now be no direct connection between Blanchardstown and Castleknock but a bus frequency — highly efficient bus service from 6 am right through to 11.30 pm and 1am on Fridays and Saturdays when the last Nitelink service runs and the new services result from extensive consultation with their customers in the area.

Dublin Bus says its Sector 7 review, which includes Blanchardstown, Castleknock, Cabra and out to Dunboyne, will now have a highly efficient bus service from 6 am right through to 11.30 pm and 1am on Fridays and Saturdays when the last Nitelink service runs and the new services result from extensive consultation with their customers in the area.

with the exception of a new key trip, the No.250.

CITY IMP — The colourful minibuses with the City Imp logo, which started operating last year on the 83 route from Kilmainage to the city is set to become a familiar sight to Dublin commuters and will soon operate from Cabra also. City Imps run every 7 minutes at peak and every 10 — 15 minutes off peak. It will also "hail and ride" in suburban areas.

239 Advertisement for Blanchardstown QBC. (*Evening Herald*, 5 April 1993, p. A8.)

240 An original Imp on O'Connell Street.

bus lanes operating from 7.00 a.m. to 7.00 p.m. with enforcement to keep cars out. The first QBC was introduced on 11 April 1993 on the route from Blanchardstown to the city centre.

Passengers were provided with an improved bus shelter with seats, and there was talk of real-time bus information, though it proved to be decades before it was available. CIÉ intended introducing 16 such QBCs, mostly radial, with a focus on the city centre, but with at least one orbital connecting the new towns. A short-lived addition was the Imp service. These were small mini-buses and designed to offer a high frequency and very flexible service, with the tag 'Go minic anseo, go tapaid ansiúd'. Once within residential areas, which they typically served, they could be hailed anywhere, reminiscent of the first years of the bus service. Their small size meant that they could work roads too narrow for conventional buses and it was anticipated that it would be possible to have them travel in pedestrianized areas, such as the potentially transformed Parliament Street. The Imps, with 23 seats and made in Donegal, were, after the almost inevitable industrial relations stand-off, introduced in April 1992 on the 83 route from Kimmage to the city centre. They were initially successful, carrying 30,000 people a week in the first year of operation, and a further 60 buses were due for introduction in 1993 to serve suburbs such as Marino and Cabra. The time period was one for innovation, with buses being given the ability to hold green lights and passengers being promised 'smart cards', to be called 'Dash', that would allow them to pay for their bus journeys. There was still talk of busways now in the form of 'guided busways'. The bus would run between guide rails with automatic steering keeping it on the correct path. Essen and Adelaide were offered as models.

Not all these initiatives worked, nor was everything introduced quite as intended but it was a clear manifestation of the shift from road building and cars to public transport and buses. There was therefore no further need for grandiose motorway plans and that era came to an end. The required co-ordination of the various agencies took some time too. By the early 1990s, there were the Dublin Transportation Task Force and the Dublin Transport Initiative but it would be a bit longer before an agency with statutory power was given a stab at sorting out Dublin's traffic once and for all.

The city at the end of the 1980s

The 1970s but more particularly, the 1980s, were decades in which people changed how they used the city. They and the city were more suburban and their routines and patterns altered to reflect this. As the 1980s progressed it seemed as if this move to the suburbs was unstoppable and inevitable. Dublin perhaps might become like some US cities, with settlement spread out over the countryside and little obvious connection with a centre. Yet, the early years of the 1990s began to suggest a change as the impact of renewal began to be felt. As a conclusion, this chapter will attempt to present a picture of the city as it moved into the 1990s.

There is no universally accepted manner of delimiting a city. Every city has a legal boundary and Dublin has several of these but these boundaries always lag behind the spread of settlement. The contiguous built-up area is a neat definition because it seeks to delimit the city in terms of its physical presence but that does not work for Dublin. It has suburbs that are physically distinct from the city but which are absolutely part of it. The hinterland concept might be useful but Dublin's hinterland by the end of the 1980s stretched far into the adjoining counties, to the extent that it would encompass much that was rural, at least in terms of business and commerce. So what is offered here is a compromise. The data are based on the built up area, whether contiguous or not, guided by the definitions used in the census of population and honed by personal experience.

The population of the built-up area of Dublin had grown to 798,230 by 1971 and it was a dominant primate city with 26.1 per cent of the national population. This was more than five times the size of Cork, the next city in the hierarchy. Growth continued during the 1970s, especially in the new suburbs of Tallaght, Clondalkin and Blanchardstown, and the city had a population of 956,125 in 1981. Tallaght had grown from a small village centre of no more than a few hundred people in 1971 to 55,104, while both Clondalkin and Blanchardstown had doubled their populations to over 14,500 and 12,000, respectively. They still had a long way to go to catch up but even then there were aspects to their structure that pointed to difficulties ahead. Growth slowed down during the 1980s, with only a modest increase of 10,800 (1.1 per cent) between 1981–6 and little change over the next five years, to give a 1991 population of 968,276. A trend towards smaller families during the 1980s was an important reason for this slow-down but there were also fewer job opportunities for young people and emigration was significant. This caused the author to suggest in a paper in 1994 that 'there are no reasons to suggest a return to rapid urban growth in the 1990s'. There was no hint, at the time, of the economic boom that was to come.

Over recent decades, the movement of people to the suburbs, combined with changes in the organization of retailing and industry, dramatically altered how the city looked. The census data capture the effect of this. During the 1980s, there was little change in the footprint of the city but the population continued its shift to the suburbs. The county borough, the area under the control of Dublin Corporation, lost 7.4 per cent of its population during the 1970s. By 1981, a total of 524,882 people lived there, compared to 567,866 a decade previously. Losses continued, even accelerated, during the 1980s. By 1986, the population had fallen to 502,749, even though the geographical size of the county borough had increased. A further loss of 5 per cent occurred during the next five years and there were 478,389 people there in 1991. This hollowing out of the city, creating what was often called a 'doughnut' city, had implications for the efficient use of resources because the decline in numbers also signalled a change in the population structure.

In contrast, the suburbs grew and Fingal and Belgard (South Dublin) increased their population by 37.7 per cent and 27.3 per cent, respectively, during the decade. The map (figure 241) shows the impact of this in more detail for the period 1986–91. In broad terms it shows population growth concentrated in peripheral suburban areas. Conversely, most of the county borough and the inner parts of Dún Laoghaire continued to lose population. The new suburbs of Blanchardstown and Clondalkin grew strongly but it is interesting to note that Tallaght, the first of the new western suburbs to develop, experienced slow growth or decline in some areas less than twenty years after it was begun – undoubtedly due to its very unbalanced age structure. Demand for new housing in desirable residential locations was good and is evident in the strong growth in middle-class locations such as Castleknock, Malahide and Foxrock.

The population losses in the county borough were concentrated, as would be expected, in the inner city. But loss was experienced also in many of the suburban areas that were developed in the 1960s and 1970s, such as Coolock, whose residents had moved into the later stages of the life cycle. There was something different going on, though. The map of population change between 1981 and 1986 shows a clear distinction between declining inner and growing

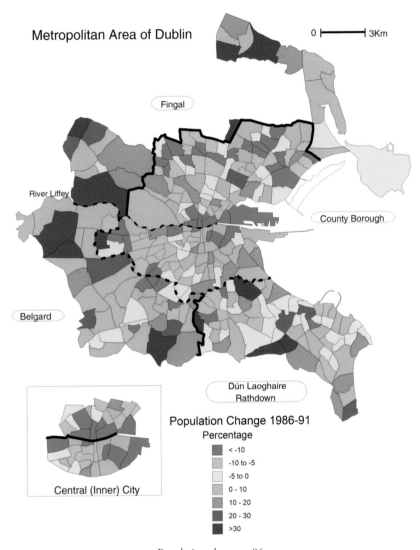

241 Population change 1986–91.

outer suburbs (Brady, 1988), something which had become blurred by 1991. During 1986–91, there was increase in parts of Sandymount and Ballsbridge while parts of Clontarf, Marino, Drumcondra and Glasnevin also grew by more than 7.5 per cent – sometimes considerably in excess of that figure. The turn-around resulted from a re-kindled interest in the inner suburbs by people who had discovered the advantages of central locations and well developed, and usually underutilized, services. For example, Marino increased

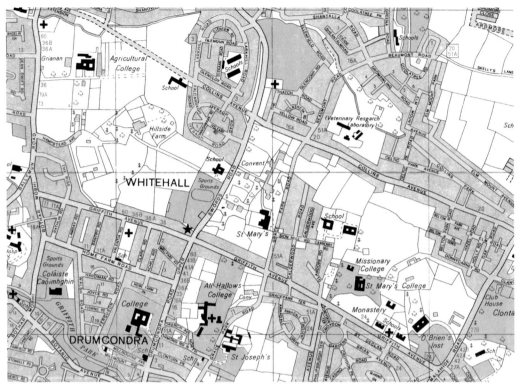

242 Undeveloped land between Griffith Avenue and Collins Avenue.
(Ordnance Survey Popular Edition, 8th edition, 1969.)

its population by 23 per cent over the five years 1986–91, wiping out a loss of over 6 per cent in the previous five years, and achieved an even greater increase of 30 per cent in the number of households. What facilitated this here (and in other locations) was a release of a substantial land bank.

In many countries, the growth of cities can be spatially irregular. For all sorts of reasons development may be uneven and bypass areas. A look at any map of Dublin prior to the 1990s showed a great deal of open space within the city. Much of this was either public parks or public or private golf courses. Schools and hospitals accounted for other green spaces but scattered across the city were properties that were private and shielded from public view. High walls or tree screens often separated the grounds from the street and many passers-by would have had no idea of what went on within the boundary or indeed the scale of the property. These were institutions of various kinds, mostly in religious hands and therefore mostly Roman Catholic in orientation. These were to be found across the city. The Passionist Fathers site at Mount Argus was extensive but there was a particular concentration of these properties in the north inner suburbs in Glasnevin and Drumcondra. There was no particular geographic reason for this, rather it reflected the patterns of land ownership in the nineteenth century and the processes that led to their transfer to the various religious orders. Occasionally, some of this property came on the market and, depending on the nature of the site, its location could prove attractive to developers. However, by the end of the 1970s and especially into the 1980s, there was a major release of these properties by religious orders who wanted or needed to dispose of assets. Those in solid, 'respectable' residential areas were of considerable value for housing.

An early opportunity for an infill development presented when a part of the Eustace estate was sold for development. The plot ran parallel to Griffith Avenue, with only a narrow entrance onto the avenue, giving no hint of the scale of development behind. Courtlands was built like a suburban estate and the houses were similar to what was being provided further from the city. This was the advertising message too. The purchaser could have the best of both worlds: 'the peaceful world of comfortable suburban living and the bustling world of the exciting city life' (*Evening Herald*, 6 October 1972, p. 15). No attempt was made to blend with the existing housing on Griffith Avenue, which was mostly red brick and the houses were mostly white stucco with a small amount of coloured brick. The houses also reflected the trend for bigger units and most were four-bedroomed and semi-detached, with good garden space to the front and rear. There was a lounge with separate dining room, eschewing the trend towards open plan, with a fitted kitchen and a coloured bathroom suite (all the rage!). The houses went on sale in early 1972 and sold well and quickly during the remainder of the year so that it was nearing completion by February 1973.

Proximity to the city, though, was not always enough to ensure development. All of the circumstances had to be right. St Vincent's school and orphanage occupied a large site in Glasnevin immediately to the north of the railway line. The OS sheet shows substantial buildings as well as very large sports grounds. Plans were in hand to develop a 15 acre (6ha) portion of the site for housing in the early 1970s as the orphanage closed. On the face of it, this should have happened quickly. The area was in Glasnevin and well served by schools, churches and shops. The newly developed Phibsborough shopping centre was only minutes away. Yet, the site was not built upon until the 1980s. The sale of the property was complicated by the fact that though the facility was run by the Christian Brothers, it was the property of the St Vincent de Paul society.

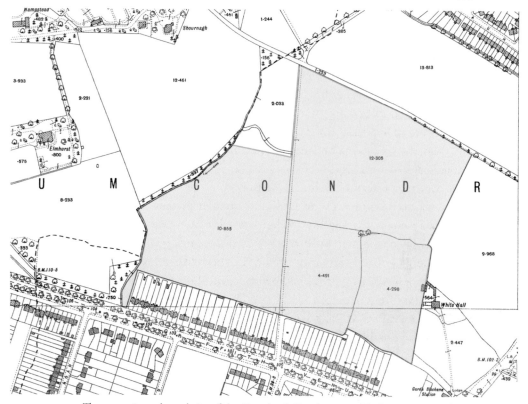

243 The approximate boundaries of the Courtlands Development. (Ordnance Survey plan, 1:2,500, Sheet 14(5) and 18(3), 1939.)

There was not yet the acceptance of infill housing that would result in the loss of amenity and the plans were opposed locally (see *Evening Herald*, 15 May 1973, p. 5). This did not prevent the sale of land but housing was not immediately built as difficulties with the site were identified. The next phase saw 7 acres purchased by the ITGWU in 1977 (*Irish Independent*, 19 August, p. 24), who obtained outline planning permission for a research and social centre in June 1978. It was not enthusiastically welcomed by the local councillor, Alice Glenn, who warned that the locals would want to see the detail of the proposal. Nothing happened and the land was sold on in 1980, reputedly for double the purchase price. It was not until the late 1980s that the environment (both financially and locally) was found to be suitable to proceed and Bovale Developments sought permission in March 1988 to clear the site and build 99 houses. Construction got underway quickly and there was steady demand for the houses even before any had been built. It was reported that ten were

244 The St Vincent's site. (Ordnance Survey plan, 1:1,100, Sheet 3197-14, 1973.)

245 The clock tower at the entrance to Dalcassian Downs.

made available in November 1988 at 'pre-construction' prices and eight were sold almost immediately (*Irish Times*, 24 November 1988, p. A5). By now, there was a clear appreciation of the virtues of living closer to the city centre in areas with well-developed services and facilities and secure reputations. The development was an immediate success.

The form of this development followed the template for such projects. No attempt was made to integrate it into the existing streetscape. Instead it was marked as being different by the building of an elaborate entrance with a clock tower. The estate was given a name that had nothing to do with the area, 'Dalcassian Downs', a strange mixture of reference to Brian Boru with a geographic feature more associated with the south of England. Advertisements promised 'homes fit for a king' in a location 'formerly inhabited by the High Kings of Ireland' (*Irish Times*, 31 March 1989, p. 26). The tradition that had emerged in the 1960s of referring to the house types by names was revived. The three-bedroomed houses were called Oak and Cedar, while the four-bedroomed version with an area of 1,200 sq. ft (111 sq. m) was called Ash. Though the development was relatively high-density, with the houses built in short terraces, using setbacks, the houses were provided with gardens ensuring a more suburban feel. However a sign of the times was the inclusion in 1990 of 'The Court', a block of 48 one- and two-bedroomed apartments.

There were not many opportunities for large infill projects like this during the 1970s. Opportunities that arose were serendipitous and, as other chapters have noted, there was no interest in building private housing in the inner city. So, the decision by many religious orders to reduce their footprints had a rapid and significant impact on the landscape, an effect that continues to the present day.

The Christian Brothers had a huge site that occupied most of the northern Griffith Avenue frontage east of Glandore Road and stretched northwards almost as far as Collins Avenue. It had been bigger. After all, Dublin Corporation's Marino scheme was built partially on land that had formed part of this estate as had the fine complex of two primary schools and the imposing parish church. In 1988, they decided that they would sell a portion of their land, mainly the back site, retaining the frontage and the imposing views the rising ground there provided. The site comprised 32 acres (13ha) and planning permission was sought in September for 421 two-storey houses. Described as being 'one of the largest residential estates planned for Dublin since the 'Seventies property boom there would be 296 semi-detached houses, 221 terraced houses and just four detached units' (*Irish Press,* 22 July 1988, p. 23).

246 Part of the extensive property of the Christian Brothers on Griffith Avenue. The housing was largely on the northern part of the site. (Ordnance Survey plan, 1:1,100, Sheets 3198-6 & 7, 1973.)

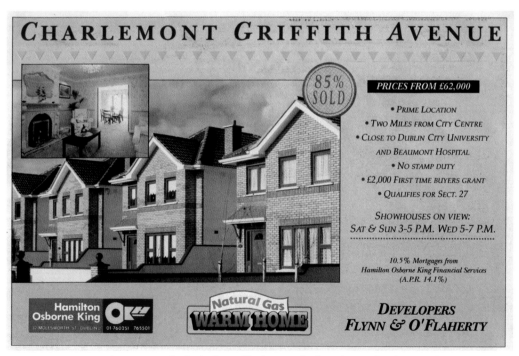

247 Advertisement for final sales at Charlemont. (*Independent*, 12 October 1990.)

248 The impressive entrance to the Charlemont development, 1989. The houses on the right are the show houses.

There would be little or no indication of the existence of the development from the main road, with only an imposing entrance indicating the sole access to Griffith Avenue. Appropriately named Charlemont, show houses were available by September 1989 for the four types of three- and four-bedroomed houses and bungalows. The layout was suburban in character – there was not yet a requirement for significantly higher plot ratios in inner suburbs – and comprised a series of culs-de-sac. It sold very rapidly and the developers claimed three weeks later that half of the houses had been sold, some sight-unseen. Undoubtedly the location was crucial to their attractiveness, but so also was their qualification under Section 27 (Section 23). They came with gas central heating, fitted kitchens and en-suite 'master bedrooms', and they followed the modern trend of having the dining room flow into the kitchen space. By October of the following year the claim was that 85 per cent had been sold (*Irish Independent*, 22 October 1990).

All Hallows Missionary College had a very large campus whose main boundary was along Grace Park Road. It also had a substantial frontage on Griffith Avenue that had escaped development in the 1920s when Marino's reserved area (see volume 2, *Dublin, 1910–1940*, pp 248–69) was in the process of joining up with that of the Drumcondra scheme. A portion of this site was

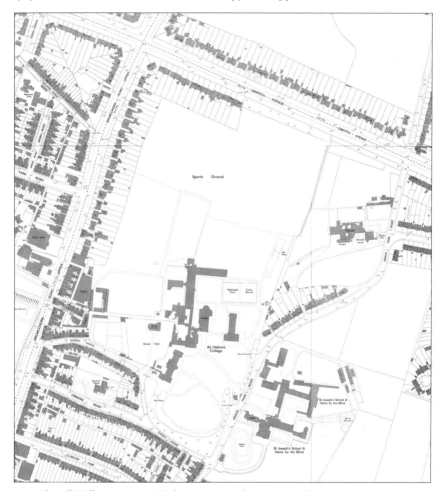

249 The All Hallows campus. (Ordnance Survey plan, 1:1,1000, Sheets 3198-1, 2, 6, 7, 1973.)

developed at about the same time as Charlemont. Part of the plot became the new home for Dominican College, which transferred from Eccles Street. The remainder became Beresford. As with Charlemont, the road frontage did not form part of the scheme except to provide an entrance to the development. This was aimed at a higher-priced market. The site was 8 acres (3.2ha) but only 63 houses were planned. All of the four- and five-bedroomed houses were detached and faced in red brick.

The prices ranged from £125,000 to £198,000, whereas the new houses in Charlemont were priced from £67,000. The kind of local amenities that it was felt useful to mention included 'marine activities at Clontarf and Howth, golf courses at Royal Dublin St Anne's and Clontarf Golf and Bowling Club'.

250 The entrance to Beresford from Griffith Avenue.

Whether it was the advertiser or the developer is unclear, but it seems that there might have been some concern about any suggestion that the location was Marino, since the headline announced 'Detached Luxury in Old Clontarf' (*Irish Independent*, 23 February 1990, p. 4). Since 'Old Clontarf' was a location or a concept unknown to anyone even in the locality, it is a testament to the tenacity of the purchasers that it could be reported that half of the houses had been sold by April (*Irish Independent*, 20 April 1990, p. 25).

A small advertisement appeared in October 1994 announcing the final phase of the development, introducing a new four-bedroomed style but at a minimum price of £115,000 (*Irish Times*, 24 October 1994).

Between Charlemont and Beresford was the grounds of High Park. As the name indicated it was on the steeply rising ground between Griffith Avenue and Collins Avenue and was an extensive campus of mixed uses. The convent of the Sisters of Our Lady of Charity presented a very striking vista to anyone passing but the presence there of a Magdalen home and laundry since 1856 had largely passed from public interest. That use only became a matter of public debate when a decision was taken in 1993 to exhume those who had been buried in the convent cemetery. So, the development of a housing scheme in 1989 did not generate the controversy that might otherwise have arisen. The

251 The three-bedroomed development at High Park. (*Irish Times*, 5 March 1992, p. A8.)

order took the decision to sell a portion of the campus for housing to fund the building of a retirement facility for the increasingly elderly women who lived there. Outline planning permission was received for a 2.3ha site at the corner of Collins Avenue and Grace Park Road in December 1989 but permission was refused for housing development on a more favourable site close to Griffith Avenue. It was some time before that obstacle could be overcome, and apartments had by then become the favoured form of housing.

The northern development ignored the possibilities that a street frontage on two major roads offered and instead decided to build inside the convent wall – right to its edge in a number of cases. The first phase of the development was a rather conventional scheme of three-bedroomed semi-detached houses, which went on sale in early March 1992 at £75,000 each. Even before the official opening it was claimed by the developers that some half of the sixty-four houses had already been sold. This generated frenetic viewing the following weekend and sales were brisk, leaving only a handful by the summer. Attention then moved to another element of the development, a scheme of

252 The Court, High Park, Gracepark Road, 1992. (*Irish Times*, 5 November 1992, p. A3.)

32 two-bedroomed units. For reasons best known to the developers these were marked off from the remainder of the scheme with an entrance and a different name. They became 'The Court, High Park, Gracepark Road'. They were unusual because of their high density; there was little green space to be seen there, whereas the three-bedroomed houses had 15m gardens. The high density was further reinforced by building them as 'back-to-back' houses. This represented a return to a style of housing that had been commonplace in the industrial slums of British cities during the middle to end of the nineteenth century. They became notorious hotbeds of infection and disease because of their lack of light and ventilation. They slowly disappeared there as improved health regulations effectively banned their construction. They were never a feature of Dublin so their sudden appearance at the beginning of the 1990s was greeted with some surprise in academic circles. They still had the same high-density characteristics of their nineteenth-century antecedents, and it was surprising that they were given planning permission. The 'back-to-back'

character generated no interest in the media; rather, it was the use of granite in the façade and the attractive price of £59,000.

These examples of infill development explain the selective turn-around in population in some areas of the inner-suburbs, which was described above. That they were essentially suburban in character demonstrates that density was not yet seen as a major issue in planning.

Population imbalance

The creation of the new suburbs in Tallaght, Clondalkin and Blanchardstown had a number of inherent difficulties, which were similar to those experienced in British new towns. Ensuring that services were supplied in line with population growth was a problem because the local authorities could only *facilitate* provision; because of their limited financial resources, they had to rely on the 'market' to provide. This ensured that provision tended to follow development, investors taking no chances, and there could be long periods of underprovision. Another area of difficulty lay in the age distribution of the population. Ideally, an area needs a well-balanced age structure so that the various services associated with different age groups are used efficiently. Imbalances create excessive demand and, if provided for, will ultimately result in excess provision.

The population pyramid for Dublin for 1971 shows that the city had quite an inbuilt growth dynamic, 41.5 per cent was under the age of 20 years. The shape of the pyramid was one associated with growth but there was a hint that matters might be changing: the proportion of very young children was less than would be expected. Despite this, the absolute numbers meant that the city was set for significant household formation during the next decade and this would produce its own natural increase in time. The 1981 pyramid showed a city that was still young, though with a small decrease in the proportion under 20 years to just under 40 per cent. The difference compared to 1971 was only marginal, a percentage point or so, but it was significant. A decrease in fertility was now restraining population growth. A standard measure of fertility is the number of children a woman in child-bearing years would be likely to have. The national estimate was 2.16 at the end of the 1980s, just above replacement rate, and it would have been lower in Dublin. This resulted in household size declining within the city from 3.94 persons in 1971 to 3.58 in 1981. This too might not seem like a dramatic decline but it signalled that Dublin's population required more housing units, more than would have been

Dublin City

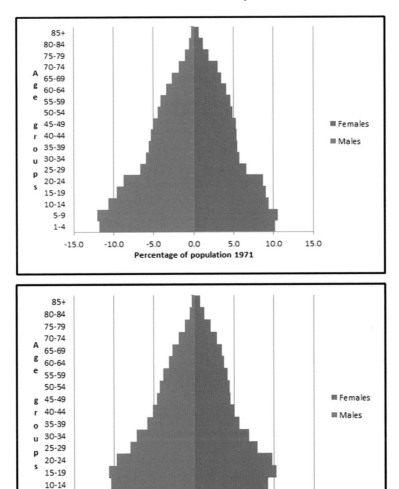

253 Population pyramids for Dublin city, 1971 and 1981.

required by a similar population in earlier generations. By 1991 the population of the city was heading into maturity. The largest population cohorts were now aged between 15 and 24 years, which accounted for 19 per cent. The city

Dublin City

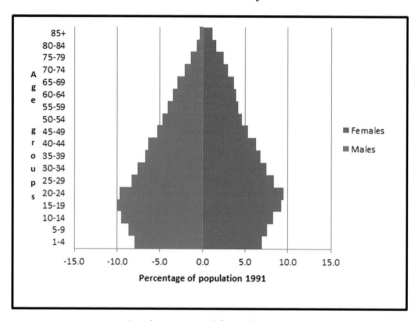

254 Population pyramid for Dublin city, 1991.

was not heading into anything like a rapid decline, fully one-third of the population was under 20 years but unless there was going to be an economic transformation that would both end emigration and make Dublin a major destination for migrants, the days of rapid growth were over. Households continued to decline in size and had fallen to 3.27 in 1991. In fact, over 43 per cent of households had two people or fewer in them. Of those families who had children at home in 1991, some 57 per cent had two children or fewer and only 7.5 per cent had five or more children. There were now 14.8 per cent more households in 1991 than in 1981 and their number had even increased in the county borough. This kept the pressure on housing supply.

The city was not a homogenous entity and the demographic structure was different in the older suburbs compared to the newer ones. Ballybough (census area Ballybough B) was one of those older areas, just outside the inner city, which lost population. The pyramid for 1981 shows an area with little potential growth, though with a significant proportion of young adults. Though 22.5 per cent was under 20 years, the proportion over the age of 50 years was 34 per cent. It was a similar picture in Clontarf (Clontarf West D), which took in much of Fairview and Marino. Here almost 39 per cent were over the age

Ballybough

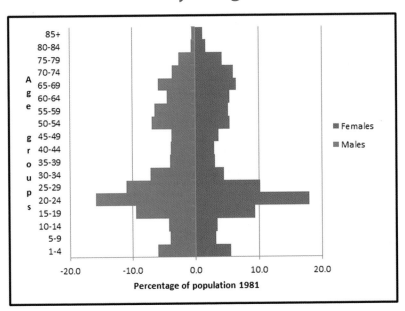

Clontarf

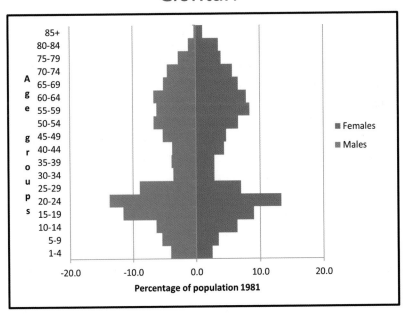

255 Population pyramids for Ballybough and Clontarf, 1981.

Tallaght 1

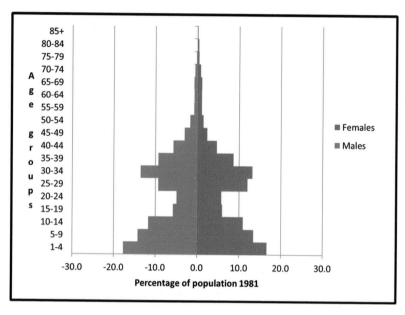

Tallaght 2

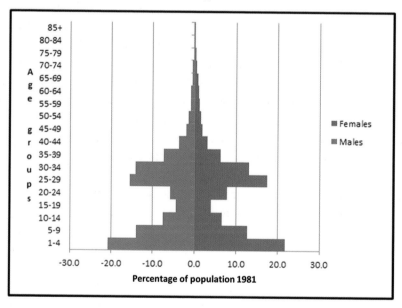

256 Population pyramids for two areas in Tallaght, 1981.

of 50, compared to just over 24 per cent under the age of 20 years. Both were areas with increasing numbers of smaller, older households.

The contrast with Tallaght could not have been more marked. The area shown here had a population of just under 13,000 in 1981 and the pyramid shows a classic picture of concentrated growth. Reflecting the rapid development of the 1970s, 41.6 per cent were under the age of 14 years. Younger children dominated, with three times as many aged under 5 years compared to those aged 10–14 years. Their parents accounted for the greater part of the remaining population, with 36.9 per cent aged between 25 and 40 years. There were hardly any older people in the area. This picture was repeated in the other areas of Tallaght and was emerging in Blanchardstown and Clondalkin. This imbalance caused problems in resource allocation from the very beginning. Primary schools were needed almost immediately but provision could not keep up with population growth. This resulted in temporary solutions that persisted for many years and class sizes far in excess of what was acceptable, even in a country where class sizes were acknowledged to be too large. By the end of the 1970s, there were over 20 primary schools in Tallaght but this was not enough. At the same time, schools in other parts of the city were operating well below capacity. This problem was widespread from Foxrock to Ballyfermot. For example, a meeting of parents in Ballyfermot took place to express concern about the financial viability of the schools in their areas in May 1982. At the meeting it was noted that schools that now catered for 1,500 students had once catered for 5,000 students (*Evening Herald*, 17 May 1982, p. 4). There were occasional suggestions of busing students from Tallaght and Clondalkin to places with capacity, but these never came to much, with neither parents nor the state expressing much enthusiasm. By the early 1980s, the problem was moving to second level, with primary schools finding that there were no local secondary schools with capacity. A different form of 'busing' resulted, with parents embarking on long school runs, the inadequacy of the bus system being another problem. Despite the scale of the issue, it got relatively little traction outside the immediate area. The blunt truth was that education funding was in crisis generally, as part of the economic doldrums in which the state found itself in the early 1980s. It was left pretty much to solve itself, which it did eventually as class sizes and class numbers came more into balance with capacity.

The pyramids for 1991 show that not much had changed in Ballybough and Clontarf. Ballybough's population was more or less the same and there had been an injection of younger couples, which retained the population distribution.

Ballybough

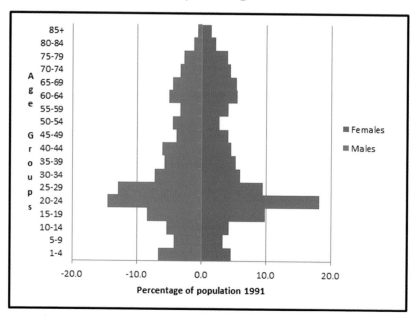

Clontarf

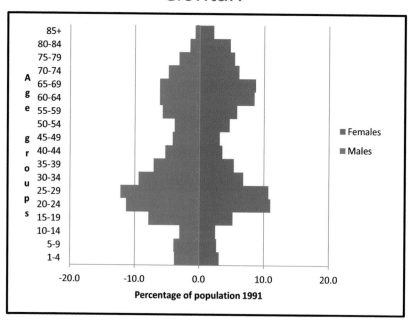

257 Population pyramids for Ballybough and Clontarf, 1991.

Jobstown

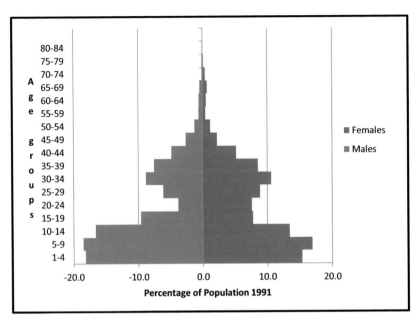

Belgard

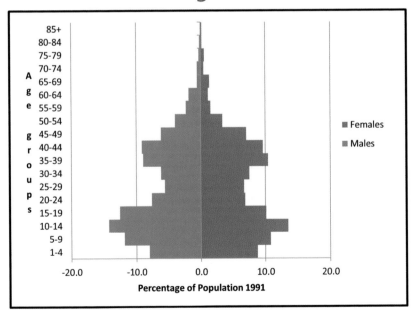

258 Population pyramids for Jobstown and Belgard in Tallaght, 1991.

Clontarf had become older, sitting on a narrower base of children. The census areas had changed in Tallaght for 1991 so a direct comparison with 1981 is not possible. Jobstown shows that growth was continuing in some areas but the narrowing of the base of the pyramid in Belgard shows that maturity had arrived there. The days of rapid growth had been short and intense but now they were over.

Housing stock

The apartment boom was only part of a significant increase in the housing stock. The footprint of the city continued to expand. The table below shows the age of the housing stock in Dublin in 1971. Over 7,000 units dated from before the middle of the nineteenth century. A further 24,000 units dated to second half of that century, most of them, as would be expected, concentrated in the county borough. Most of Dublin's housing was newer, with more than 52 per cent built after 1940. The suburbanization of the southern suburbs is clearly noticeable in the 75 per cent built since 1960, a characteristic shared with neighbouring Dún Laoghaire.

Table 12. Age of housing stock in Dublin as of 1971.

Period	Dublin	County borough	North suburbs	South suburbs	Dún Laoghaire
Pre-1860	7,101	5,312	1,253	101	435
1860–99	23,590	19,769	2,834	133	854
1900–18	16,524	14,209	1,418	103	794
1919–40	37,310	31,553	2,785	237	2,735
1941–60	54,242	37,106	3,267	568	1,301
1961+	40,589	19,056	1,725	3,553	16,255

By 1981, the impact of continuing suburbanization, combined with some inner-city clearance, ensured that while there were still 41,698 units from before 1919, these accounted for 17 per cent of the stock while just over a quarter (65,703) had been built since 1970. By 1991, just under 40 per cent (115,589 units) were post-1970, though a slowdown was evident during the 1980s. There was still quite an amount of older housing, though the total had diminished to 37,293. The massive growth in new building ensured that this now accounted for only 13.3 per cent of the total. In 1971, the census reported 179,404 dwellings in the city but there were now 286,300, most of which housed a single family.

Table 13. Age of housing stock in Dublin city as of 1991.

Period	Total	Percentage
Pre-1919	37,293	13.3
1919–40	34,350	12.2
1940–60	55,459	19.7
1960–70	42,587	15.1
1970–80	64,947	23.1
1980–5	26,880	9.6
Post-1986	19,742	7.0
Not stated	5,042	1.8

Compared to the remainder of Ireland, Dubliners had been relatively slow in becoming home owners. It was only in the 1960s, with relative improvements in income and better access to mortgages that this process accelerated. Dublin Corporation had continued during the 1960s to be a major housing provider and figures provided to the Council in early 1969 showed that they had provided 51,878 dwellings to date, of which 5,944 had been provided in the five years to 31 March 1968. The Ballymun project had helped ensure that there had been almost an equality in flat building versus house building; 2,874 versus 3,070 in recent years. Tenant purchase had been relatively slow recently and though some 5,950 dwellings from the total above were being purchased, only 848 had been sold in the previous five years. Of these, 225 were new houses and 623 were sales to existing tenants (Dublin Corporation Minutes, 3 February 1969). This was about to change.

In 1967, in return for providing a solution to the decades-long issue with differential rents, the minister for local government, Kevin Boland, required Dublin Corporation to put a housing sales process in place without delay. Despite vigorous public opposition to the process that emerged, the tenants quietly and in large numbers availed of the offer and became property owners. By August 1970, there had been 9,810 applications to purchase. Market values had been agreed in 3,976 cases and purchase completed in 2,919 instances (Report 134/1970). The take-up was hardly surprising since there was excellent value to be had. In older housing areas such as Cabra West, the houses were valued at around £1,700. Discounts for continuous tenancies could amount to over £500, resulting in net sale prices of £1,100. New housing areas were more expensive. A house in Edenmore could be valued at just over £3,000 but the discount for continuous tenancy could be as much as £790, leaving a total purchase price of just over £2,200 with a repayment period of 35 years

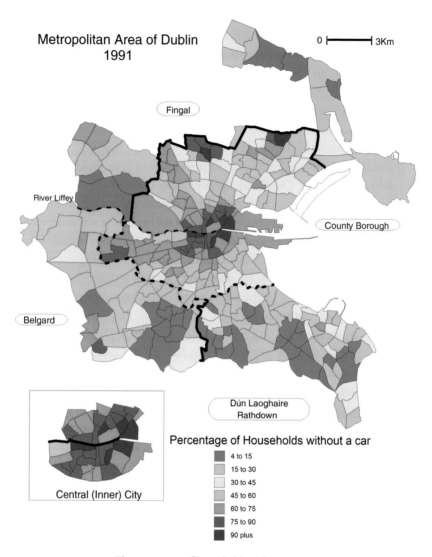

259 The percentage of households with no car, 1991.

tended to have few people in the better-paid occupations and to be more dependent on social housing.

By 1991, for the reasons described above, local-authority housing was no longer as dominant in the city as it once had been. The dark green area of the map shows where fewer than 5 per cent of the housing units, whether flats or conventional housing, were being rented from the local authority. It is a very polarized picture. The dark purple shows the other extreme, areas

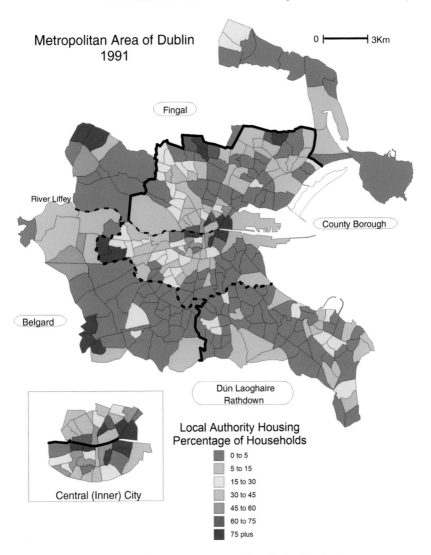

260 The percentage of housing units rented from the local authority, 1991.

where in excess of 75 per cent of housing was local authority. By 1991, these concentrations were spatially distinct and on the edge of the city in west Tallaght, Finglas, Ballymun and along the northern edge. Matters were more complex in the inner city as a result of the slum-clearance programmes of the previous decades and were set to become even more so when the apartment boom was reflected in the official figures.

Finally, the distribution of 'higher professionals' shows the most favoured residential areas in the city. This group as defined by the census comprised

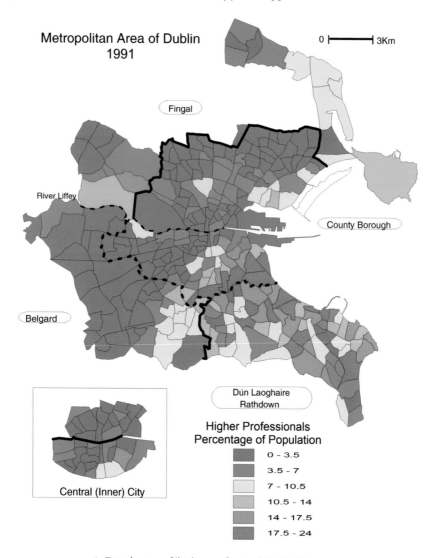

261 Distribution of 'higher professionals' in Dublin, 1991.

clergy, doctors, dentists, chemists, university academics, accountants, lawyers, judges and similar occupations. The census estimated that just under 55,000 people (or about 5.6 per cent) were in that category; the entire household being categorized on the basis of the person first named in the census. The colour differences shows how polarized the city was. The green areas were those with fewer people in these social groups; the darker the shade, the lower the percentage. Conversely, those with higher concentrations are shown in

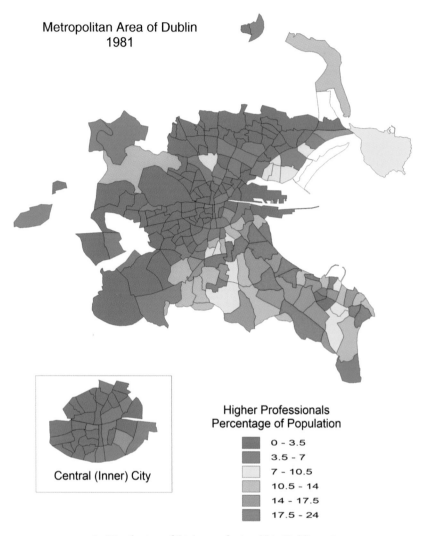

Metropolitan Area of Dublin
1981

Central (Inner) City

Higher Professionals
Percentage of Population

■ 0 - 3.5
■ 3.5 - 7
□ 7 - 10.5
▨ 10.5 - 14
▨ 14 - 17.5
■ 17.5 - 24

262 Distribution of 'higher professionals' in Dublin, 1981.

deeper shades of pink. The percentages ranged from almost zero to just under 24 per cent. The south-eastern sector was the most favoured part of the city by the higher professionals and there is nothing surprising in this. This has been the favoured location for the middle classes since the early years of the nineteenth century, when the move to the suburbs first began. The most favoured locations, those with the deepest pink colours, included Ballsbridge, Foxrock and Killiney. That is not to say that there were no favoured areas on the northside but the map shows that they were fewer and the concentration less intense. People in this group could be found in Castleknock, Clontarf, Howth and in the newly developed suburbs of Malahide and Portmarnock. The final map shows the distribution of higher professionals in 1981. The census areas are different so a direct comparison is not possible but the pattern is the same. Higher professionals comprised just under 7 per cent of the city's population so the concentration in the south-east was quite marked. At the other end of the scale, the huge swathe of green shows the parts of the city where very few fell into that social group (see also Brady and Parker, 1986). Much might have changed in Dublin since 1970 but much had also stayed the same.

Sources and bibliography

Sources

This volume builds on the topics developed in the seven previous volumes of the series and especially the four volumes that deal with Dublin in the twentieth century. The reader is encouraged to explore these volumes in building up a comprehensive view of the city.

- *Dublin through space and time, c.900–1900*
- *Dublin, 1910–1940: shaping the city and suburbs*
- *Dublin, 1745–1922: hospitals, spectacle and vice*
- *Dublin docklands reinvented: the post-industrial regeneration of a European city quarter*
- *Dublin, 1930–1950: the emergence of the modern city*
- *Dublin, 1950–1970: houses, flats and high rise*
- *Dublin in the 1950s and 1960s: cars, shops and suburbs*

For a finer level of granularity and detailed study of individual buildings, the reader is directed to the series edited by Ellen Rowley, More than Concrete Blocks, published by Dublin City Council and Four Courts Press.

This volume was as reliant as ever on maps to illustrate the ideas being discussed. The revision of the 25 inch (1:2,500) series of Ordnance Survey plans was complete by the mid-1940s and they were not revised again. Local revisions were produced by organizations such as Dublin Corporation but they were not for public release and the quality of the output, though sufficient for their purpose, was variable. These OS maps remain useful for many parts of the city, even during the timescale of this book because relatively little happened to the urban landscape. They were replaced by the 1:1,000 series towards the end of the 1960s and this meant that there was now a highly detailed map resource available. The issue was that they were too detailed and too many sheets were needed to look at even a small urban area. Nonetheless they proved very useful to this volume and the reader is asked to ignore the obvious joins between sheets. In the 1930s the Ordnance Survey began to produce its Popular Edition maps of the city of Dublin at a convenient scale. There is a provisional edition (265b) dated 1933 and then an edition at 1:25,000, which has an imprint of 1948. Publication of these maps became a more regular feature during the 1960s and 1970s and they provide a very useful overview of suburban development. The degree of revision varied from edition to edition and it is important not to assume that the printing date means that the map is current as of that date. The scale of maps also varied from 1:25,000 to 1:18,000. This is not a major issue but it means that temporal comparisons sometimes require some digital manipulation. As the city began to grow so the 1:63,360 sheet of the Dublin District became more useful and the number of editions allow the expansion of the city to be seen. The scale later changed to 1:50,000 but that will only need to be considered in a subsequent volume. To these must be added the extremely useful Geographia plans, which provide a view of the city at a scale of 4 inches to the mile (about 1:15,800).

Previous volumes have made considerable use of the variety of guidebooks that were produced. The 1970s and 1980s were not great decades for these sources and only a very few were produced with the kind of detail that facilitates geographical investigation. The Ward Lock guides were no more and the city was no longer producing its detailed 'official guides'. Thom's street directories were still published but the detail provided was greatly reduced, almost to the bare minimum. Likewise with the Goad Fire Insurance plans. Gone was the day when these maps provided significant detail about the uses of most of the city centre. The current offerings were produced on flimsy dyeline paper and the city centre covered in two sheets.

The other great loss was *Dublin Opinion*. This magazine's cartoons had proved an invaluable resource since the 1920s. Not only were they fascinating in their own right, they also provided a window onto the issues that were bothering the citizens of Dublin and provided at least one perspective on those issues. It ceased publication in 1968 and though a number of attempts were made at revival in the 1970s, these did not provide the same insights as previously.

The reader will notice that there are fewer postcards reproduced in this volume compared to the earlier volumes. The range of images available continued to shrink during the 1970s and into the 1980s and there were few of the more eclectic views of the city. Censuses were undertaken in 1971, 1979, 1981, 1986 and 1991. The CSO continued the practice, first adopted in 1971, of reporting much of the information at a small spatial scale – the district electoral division. By the end of the 1980s, the city was described by almost 300 of these units.

As noted in previous volumes, the debates in the Oireachtas are an important source, especially the discussions during the second stage of legislation. Not only were the various political viewpoints outlined, statistical data were often provided that would be difficult to obtain from another source. The archives of the *Irish Times*, *Irish Press* and *Irish Independent* and a host of local newspapers are now available electronically. The search engines are a lot better than previously, though many queries can be 'hit or miss'. Another repository of great use is the City Archive, maintained by Dublin Corporation. Of particular note and value is the set of printed reports of the meetings of the Council and its Committees, referred to in the form Report XX/19XX. While the political commentary can be anodyne, the range of statistics and information recorded is astonishing.

Bibliography

Aalen, F.H.A. and Whelan, K. (eds) (1992) *Dublin city and county: from prehistory to present*. Dublin: Geography Publications.
Abercrombie, P. (1944) *Great London plan*. London: Stationery Office.

Abercrombie, P. and Forshaw, J.H. (1943) *The county of London plan*. UK: Macmillan and Company Ltd.

Abercrombie, P., Duffy, G. and Giron, L.F. (1942) The Dublin Town Plan [with comments], *Studies: An Irish Quarterly Review*, 31(122), pp 155–70.

Abercrombie, P., Kelly, S. and Kelly, A. (1922) *Dublin of the future: the new town plan*. Liverpool: University Press of Liverpool.

Abercrombie, P., Kelly, S. and Robertson, M. (1941) *Dublin sketch development plan*. Dublin: Dublin Corporation.

Abrams, C. (1961) Urban renewal project in Ireland (Dublin), prepared for the Government of Ireland by Charles Abrams, appointed under the United Nations Programme of Technical Assistance. NY: United Nations.

An Foras Forbartha (1971) *Transportation in Dublin*. Dublin: An Foras Forbartha.

An Foras Forbartha (1972) *Dublin transportation study: technical reports*. Dublin: An Foras Forbartha.

Bailey, M.L. (1983) *Air quality in Ireland: recent trends in atmospheric emissions and concentrations*. WR/C85. Dublin: An Foras Forbartha.

Bailey, M.L., Bowman, J.J. and O'Donnell, C. (1986) *Air quality in Ireland: the present position*. WR/G13. Dublin: An Foras Forbartha.

Ballymun Amenity Group (1974) *Ballymun: the experiment that failed*. Dublin: Ballymun Amenity Group.

Bannon, M.J. (1973) *Office location in Ireland and the role of central Dublin*. Dublin: An Foras Forbartha.

Bannon, M.J. (1978) Patrick Geddes and the emergence of modern town planning in Ireland, *Irish Geography*, 11(2), pp 141–8.

Bannon, M.J. (ed.) (1985a) *The emergence of Irish planning, 1880–1920*. Dublin: Turoe Press.

Bannon, M.J. (1985b) The genesis of modern Irish planning. *In:* Bannon, M.J. (ed.) *The emergence of Irish planning, 1880–1920*. Dublin: Turoe Press, pp 189–260.

Bannon, M.J. (ed.) (1989a) *Planning: the Irish experience, 1920–1988*. Dublin: Wolfhound Press.

Bannon, M.J. (1989b) Irish planning from 1921 to 1945. *In:* Bannon, M.J. (ed.) *Planning: the Irish experience, 1920–1988*. Dublin: Wolfhound Press, pp 13–70.

Bannon, M.J., Eustace, J. and O'Neill, M. (1981) *Urbanisation: problems of growth and decay in Dublin*. Report 55. Dublin: National Economic and Social Council.

Behan, D. (1965) *My brother Brendan*. London: Leslie Frewin.

Bolger, D. (ed.) (1988) *Invisible cities, the new Dubliners: a journey through unofficial Dublin*. Dublin: Raven Arts Press.

Bowley, M. (1945) *Housing and the state, 1919–1944*. London: Allen & Unwin.

Boyd, G. (2006) *Dublin, 1745–1922: hospitals, spectacle and vice*. Dublin: Four Courts Press.

Brady, J. (1986) The impact of clean air legislation on Dublin households, *Irish Geography*, 19, pp 41–4.

Brady J. (1988) Population change in Dublin, 1981–1986, *Irish Geography*, 21(1), pp 41–4.

Brady, J. (1994) Dublin – change and challenge. *In:* Clout, H. (ed.) *Europe's cities in the late twentieth century*. Netherlands Geographical Studies 176, pp 69–84.

Brady, J. (2001a) Dublin in the nineteenth century – an introduction. *In:* Brady, J. and Simms, A. (eds), *Dublin through space and time*. Dublin: Four Courts Press, pp 159–65.

Brady, J. (2001b) Dublin at the turn of the century. *In:* Brady, J. and Simms, A. (eds), *Dublin through space and time*. Dublin: Four Courts Press, pp 221–81.

Brady, J. (2001c) The heart of the city – commercial Dublin, *c.*1890–1915. *In:* Brady, J. and Simms, A. (eds), *Dublin through space and time*. Dublin: Four Courts Press, pp 282–340.

Brady, J. (2004) Reconstructing Dublin city centre in the 1920s. *In:* Clarke, H., Prunty, J. and Hennessy, M. (eds) *Surveying Ireland's past: multidisciplinary essays in honour of Anngret Simms*. Dublin: Geography Publications, pp 639–64.

Brady, J. (2005) Geography as she used to be, *Geographical Viewpoint*, 31, pp 29–39.

Brady, J. (2006) Dublin – growth and economic prosperity 1995–2005. Archived paper for XIV International Economic History Congress. Helsinki. http://www.helsinki.fi/iehc2006/papers3/Brady.pdf.

Brady, J. (2014) *Dublin, 1930–1950: the emergence of the modern city*. Dublin: Four Courts Press.

Brady J. (2015) The Liffey and a bridge too far: bridge-building and governance in Dublin, 1870–1960, *Irish Geography*, 47(2), 75–103.

Brady, J. (2015) Dublin – a city of contrasts. *In:* Fogarty, A. and O'Rourke, F. (eds) *Voices on Joyce*. Dublin: UCD Press, pp 77–95.

Brady, J. (2016) *Dublin, 1950–1970: houses, flats and high rise*. Dublin: Four Courts Press.

Brady, J. (2017) *Dublin in the 1950s and 1960s: cars, shops and suburbs*. Dublin: Four Courts Press.

Brady, J. and Parker, A.J. (1975) The factorial ecology of Dublin – a preliminary investigation, *Economic and Social Review*, 7(4), pp 35–54.

Brady, J. and Parker, A.J. (1986) The socio-demographic structure of Dublin 1981, *Economic and Social Review*, 17(4), pp 229–52.

Brady, J. and Simms, A. (eds) (2001) *Dublin through space and time*. Dublin: Four Courts Press.

Brady, J.V. (1917) *The future of Dublin – practical slum reform*. Dublin: Dollard.

Brooke, H. (1952) *Living in flats: report of the flats subcommittee of the central housing advisory committee*. London: HMSO.

Buchanan, C. (1963a) *Traffic in towns* – A study of the long term problems of traffic in urban areas – reports of the steering group and working group appointed by the minister of transport. London: HMSO.

Buchanan, C. (1963b) *Traffic in towns*. The specially shortened edition of the Buchanan report. UK: Penguin.

Buchanan, Colin and Partners (1968) *Regional studies in Ireland*. Dublin: An Foras Forbartha.

Cabot, D. (ed.) (1985) *The state of the environment*. Dublin: An Foras Forbartha.

Coal Information Services (1985) Towards a planned improvement in Dublin's air quality. Dublin: Coal Information Services.

Corpus Christi Parish (1991) *Golden jubilee, 1941–1991* [private publication, no details].

Costello, P. and Farmar, T. (1992) *The very heart of the city: the story of Denis Guiney and Clerys.* Dublin: A&A Farmar.

Cullinan, Eve-Anne (ed.) (1992) *Development programme for Temple Bar.* Dublin: Temple Bar Properties.

Custom House Docks (1986). *Custom House Docks Dublin planning scheme.* Dublin: Custom House Docks Development Authority.

Daly, M.E. (1984) *Dublin: the deposed capital, a social and economic history, 1860–1914.* Cork: Cork University Press.

Dawson, J.A. (ed.) (1980) *Retail geography.* UK: Croom Helm.

Dawson, J.A. (1983) *Shopping centre development.* Topics in Applied Geography. UK: Longman.

Delaney, P. (ed.) (1975) *Dublin: a city in crisis.* Dublin: Royal Institute of the Architects of Ireland.

Department of the Environment (1995) *Guidelines on residential developments in urban renewal designated tax incentive areas.* Dublin: Department of Environment.

Dixon, D. (2014) *Dublin: the making of a capital city.* UK: Profile Books.

Douglas, R.M. (2009) *Architects of the resurrection: ailtirí na haiséirghe and the fascist 'new order' in Ireland.* UK: Manchester University Press.

Dublin Corporation (1975) Shopping in Dublin: an analysis of existing provision and a projection of future requirements. Working Paper No. 8, Draft Development Plan.

Dublin Corporation (1976) 'Dublin City Development Plan – draft review'. Unpublished.

Dublin Corporation (1980) *Dublin City Development Plan, 1980.* Dublin: Dublin Corporation.

Egan, M.J. (1961) *The parish of St Columba, Iona Road, Glasnevin* [private publication].

ERDO (1985a) *Eastern Region settlement strategy, 2011.* Main Report. Dublin: Eastern Region Development Organisation.

ERDO (1985b) *Eastern Region settlement strategy, 2011.* Summary Report. Dublin: Eastern Region Development Organisation.

Evans, H. (ed.) (1972) *New towns: the British experience.* UK: Charles Knight.

Ferriter, D. (2006) *What if? Alternative views of twentieth-century Ireland.* Ireland: Gill & Macmillan.

Ferriter, D. (2007) *Judging Dev: a reassessment of the life and legacy of Eamon de Valera.* Dublin: Royal Irish Academy.

Ferriter, D. (2010) *The transformation of Ireland, 1900–2000.* UK: Profile Books.

Festinger, L., Schachter, S. and Back, K. (1950) The spatial ecology of group formation. *In:* Festinger, L., Schachter, S. and Back, K. (eds) *Social pressure in informal groups*, pp 33–59.

Finnerty, J.F. (1898; 1920). *Ireland in pictures.* USA: Hyland.

Graeves, J. (ed.) *Temple Bar lives! A record of the architectural framework competition.* Dublin: Temple Bar Properties, 1991.

Greater Dublin Commission (1926) *Report of the greater Dublin commission of inquiry.* Dublin: Stationery Office.

Guild, R. (1989) *The Victorian house book*. New York: Rizzoli.

Hall, Mr and Mrs S.C. (1841–3) *Ireland: its scenery, character etc...* Three volumes. London: How & Parsons.

Hall, P. (2002) *Cities of tomorrow*. Oxford: Blackwell Publishing.

Hanna, E. (2013) *Modern Dublin: urban change and the Irish past, 1957–1973*. UK: Oxford University Press.

Harkness, D. and O'Dowd, M. (1981) *The town in Ireland*. Belfast: Appletree Press.

Harvey, J. (1949) *Dublin: a study in environment*. London: Batsford.

Haverty, A. (1995) *Elegant times: a Dublin story*. Dublin: Sonas.

Hay, A.M., Johnston, R.J. and Parker, A.J. (1981). Variations in grocery prices within Dublin: some tests of their stability, *Irish Geography*, 14(1), pp 91–8.

Horner, A.A. (1985) The Dublin region 1880–1980. *In:* Bannon, M.J. (ed.) *The emergence of Irish planning, 1880–1920*. Dublin: Turoe Press, pp 21–76.

Horner, A.A. (1992) From city to city-region – Dublin from the 1930s to the 1990s. *In:* Aalen, F.H.A. and Whelan, K. (eds), *Dublin city and county*. Dublin: Geography Publications, pp 327–58.

Horsey, M. (1990) *Tenements and towers: Glasgow working-class housing, 1890–1990*. UK: HMSO.

Housing Inquiry (1885) *Report of the royal commission appointed to inquire into the housing of the working classes*. Minutes of evidence etc., Ireland, British Parliamentary Papers, cd. 4547, London.

Housing Inquiry (1914) *Report of the departmental committee appointed by the Local Government Board for Ireland to inquire into the housing conditions of the working classes in the city of Dublin*. British Parliamentary Papers, 19, 1914, cd.7272/7317-xix, London.

Howard, E. (1898) *Tomorrow: a peaceful path to real reform*. London: Swan Sonnenschein.

Hoyt, H. (1939) The structure and growth of residential areas in American cities. Washington DC: Federal Housing Administration.

Hyland, J.S. (Ltd) (1898) *Ireland in pictures*. Chicago: J.S. Hyland and Co.

Igoe, V. (1990) *James Joyce's Dublin houses*. London: Mandarin Paperbacks.

Johnston, M. (1985) *Around the banks of Pimlico*. Dublin: Attic Press.

Kelly, P. (1990) Drumcondra, Clonliffe and Glasnevin township, 1878–1900. *In:* Kelly, J. and MacGearailt, U. (eds), *Dublin and Dubliners*. Dublin: Educational Company of Ireland, pp 36–51.

Kennedy, T. (ed.) (1980) *Victorian Dublin*. Dublin: Albertine Kennedy Publishing.

Killen, J. (1992) Transport in Dublin: past, present and future. *In:* Aalen, F.H.A. and Whelan, K. (eds) *Dublin city and county*. Dublin: Geography Publications, pp 305–25.

Kostof, S. (1991) *The city assembled: elements of urban form through history*. London: Thames & Hudson.

Kostof, S. (1992) *The city shaped: urban patterns and meanings through history*. London: Thames & Hudson.

Lichfield and Associates (1966) *Preliminary appraisal of shopping centre redevelopment in Dublin centre*. Report No. 1. London: Nathaniel Lichfield and Associates.

Local Government (1938) *Report of the Local Government (Dublin) Tribunal.* Dublin: Stationery Office.

Long, H.C. (1993) *The Edwardian house.* Manchester: Manchester University Press.

Luddy, M. (1995) *Women in Ireland, 1800–1918, a documentary history.* Cork: Cork University Press.

MacLaren, A. (1993) *Dublin, the shaping of a capital.* London: Belhaven Press.

Malone, P. (1990) *Office development in Dublin, 1960–1990.* UK: University of Manchester.

Martin, L.C. (1976) *Dublin in decay.* Dublin: Cobblestone Press.

McCartney, D. (1999) *UCD: a national idea: the history of University College, Dublin.* Dublin: Gill & Macmillan.

McCullough, N. (1989) *Dublin: an urban history.* Dublin: Anne Street Press.

McDonald, F. (1985) *The destruction of Dublin.* Dublin: Gill & Macmillan.

McManus, R. (1996) Public utility societies, Dublin Corporation and the development of Dublin, 1920–1940, *Irish Geography*, 29(1), pp 27–37.

McManus, R. (1998) The Dundalk Premier public utility society, *Irish Geography*, 31(2), pp 75–87.

McManus, R. (1999) The 'Building Parson' – the role of Reverend David Hall in the solution of Ireland's early twentieth-century housing problems, *Irish Geography*, 32(2), pp 87–98.

McManus, R. (2002) *Dublin, 1910–1940: shaping the city and suburbs.* Dublin: Four Courts Press.

McManus, R. (2004) The role of public utility societies in Ireland, 1919–40. *In:* Clarke, H., Prunty, J. and Hennessy, M. (eds) *Surveying Ireland's past: multidisciplinary essays in honour of Anngret Simms.* Dublin: Geography Publications, pp 613–38.

McManus, R. (2005) *'Such Happy Harmony': early twentieth-century co-operation to solve Dublin's housing problems.* Dublin: Dublin City Public Libraries.

McManus, R. (2006) The growth of Drumcondra, 1875–1940. *In:* Kelly, J. (ed.) *St Patrick's College, Drumcondra, 1875–2000: a history.* Dublin: Four Courts Press, pp 41–66.

McManus, R. (2008) *Crampton built.* Dublin: G.&T. Crampton.

McManus, R. (2011) Suburban and urban housing in the twentieth century, *Proceedings of the Royal Irish Academy*, 111C, pp 253–86.

McManus, R. (2012) 'Decent and artistic homes' – housing Dublin's middle classes in the 20th century, *Dublin Historical Record*, 65(1 & 2), pp 96–109.

McManus, R. (2012) Upper Buckingham Street: a microcosm of Dublin, 1788–2012 (with Sinead O'Shea), *Studia Hibernica*, pp 141–79.

McManus, R. (2013a) An introduction to Dublin's first citizens (with Lisa-Marie Griffith). *In:* McManus, R. and Griffith, L. (eds) *Leaders of the city: Dublin's first citizens, 1500–1950.* Dublin: Four Courts Press, pp 15–34.

McManus, R. (2013b) Lord Mayor Laurence O'Neill, Alderman Tom Kelly and Dublin's housing crisis. *In:* McManus, R. and Griffith, L. (2013) *Leaders of the city: Dublin's first citizens, 1500–1950.* Dublin: Four Courts Press, pp 141–51.

Meenan, J. (1957) Dublin in the Irish economy. *In:* Meenan, J. and Webb, D. (eds), *A view of Ireland.* Dublin: British Association for the Advancement of Science.

Talja, S. (2014) *Sport, recreation and space in urban policy. Helsinki and Dublin from the 1940s to the 1980s*. Historical Studies from the University of Helsinki XXXIII. Finland: Helsinki.

Tarn, J.N. (1973) *Five per cent philanthropy*. Cambridge: Cambridge University Press.

Taylor, N. (1973) *The village in the city*. London: Temple Smith in association with New Society.

Telesis Consultancy (1982) A *review of industrial policy*. Report 56. Dublin: National Economic and Social Council.

Tetlow, J. and Goss, A. (1965) *Homes, towns and traffic*. UK: Faber and Faber.

Tierney, S.L. (1949) Note on the occurrence of non-frontal fog or mist at Dublin airport during the period October to February. Department of Industry and Commerce Meteorological Service. Technical Note 10.

Timms, D. (1971) *The urban mosaic: towards a theory of residential differentiation*. UK: Cambridge University Press.

Tudor Walters Report (1918) *Report of the committee appointed by the president of the Local Government Board and the secretary for Scotland to consider questions of building construction in connection with the provision of dwellings for the working classes in England, Wales and Scotland*. London: HMSO.

Unwin, R. (1912) *Nothing gained by overcrowding*. London: Garden Cities and Town Planning Association.

Unwin, R. and Parker, B. (1909; 1994) *Town planning in practice*. Princeton: Princeton Architectural Press.

Watchorn, F. (1985) *Crumlin and the way it was*. Dublin: O'Donoghue Press International.

Ward Lock (1918) *A pictorial and descriptive guide to Dublin and the Wicklow tours*. 20th edition, revised. UK: Ward Lock and Company.

Wilkins, E.T. (1954) Air pollution and the London fog of December 1952, *Journal of the Royal Sanitary Institute*, 74(1), pp 1–21.

Whelan, Y. (2001a) Scripting national memory: the Garden of Remembrance, Parnell Square, *Irish Geography*, 34(1), pp 11–33.

Whelan, Y. (2001b) Symbolising the state: the iconography of O'Connell Street, Dublin after independence (1922), *Irish Geography*, 34(2), pp 145–50.

Wright, L. and Browne, K. (1974) 'A future for Dublin'. Special Issue, *Architectural Review*, Nov., pp 268–330.

Wright, M. (1963) *The Dublin region: advisory regional plan and final report*. Dublin: Stationery Office.

Illustrations

Unless otherwise indicated in the captions, images are by the author.

Index

Page numbers in *italics* refer to illustrations.